McCALL-CRABBS
Standard Test Lessons in Reading

Book B

WILLIAM A. McCALL, Ph.D.
Professor Emeritus of Education
Teachers College, Columbia University

LELAH CRABBS SCHROEDER, Ph.D.
Formerly Assistant Professor of Education
Teachers College, Columbia University

Revised under the editorial supervision of
ROBERT P. STARR. Ed.D.

TEACHERS COLLEGE PRESS
TEACHERS COLLEGE | COLUMBIA UNIVERSITY
NEW YORK AND LONDON

In my daydreams, I travel. I would love to see all the countries in the world.

I used to wish that I could walk to another country. Then at the end of the day, I could say, "I was in a foreign country today."

I've done it now. There is a bridge between El Paso, Texas, and Juarez in Mexico. Most people cross in cars, but they may also walk. I find this walk exciting. Just off the bridge in Mexico is the Avenue Juarez. Colorful stores line this busy street. Tiles, woven bags, and hand-blown glass are sold. I hear Spanish all around me. I walk on. I cross a park. Past the park is a famous mission church.

A line is painted on the sidewalk on the bridge. It marks the international boundary. High above it fly the American flag and the Mexican flag. On my way back, I stop here. I rest one foot in each country. For a moment I am in both.

1. **Juarez is in**   Ⓐ Mexico   Ⓑ Spain   Ⓒ Texas   Ⓓ the United States
2. **Between El Paso and Juarez there is**   Ⓐ a mountain   Ⓑ an ocean   Ⓒ a fence   Ⓓ a bridge
3. **On the Avenue Juarez I hear**   Ⓐ French   Ⓑ Spanish   Ⓒ German   Ⓓ English
4. **Past the park is a famous**   Ⓐ tower   Ⓑ school   Ⓒ church   Ⓓ castle
5. **Avenue Juarez is**   Ⓐ a quiet street   Ⓑ a busy street   Ⓒ an American city   Ⓓ a store
6. **The international boundary is marked by**   Ⓐ a painted line   Ⓑ a fence   Ⓒ a store   Ⓓ a church
7. **The two flags above the bridge are**   Ⓐ American and Canadian   Ⓑ American and Spanish   Ⓒ Mexican and American   Ⓓ Mexican and Canadian
8. **This story is mainly about**   Ⓐ walking to another country   Ⓑ shopping in Mexico   Ⓒ speaking Spanish   Ⓓ a famous mission church

No. right	1	2	3	4	5	6	7	8
G score	3.1	3.4	3.6	3.8	4.0	4.3	4.6	4.8

2

One morning, before the school bell rang, a little boy fell on the playground. He cried, "My arm is hurt!" Several children saw him lying on the ground. They all rushed over to help.

"We should carry him into the school," Linda said. "Peter and I are strong enough."

"No!" said Cathy. "He should not be moved, except by someone who knows first aid."

"I'll get the school nurse," Carlos said. "He'll know what to do." Then Carlos ran quickly into the school.

The nurse put the boy's arm into a splint. "Cathy was right," he said. "This child's arm was badly broken. Moving him would have made it much worse. Now the arm can be set easily. It will heal quickly."

1. **The hurt boy was** Ⓐ home in bed Ⓑ lying on the ground Ⓒ moved by Cathy and Carlos Ⓓ carrying someone
2. **The boy had broken his** Ⓐ leg Ⓑ splint Ⓒ nose Ⓓ arm
3. **Carlos looked for the nurse** Ⓐ inside the school Ⓑ on the playground Ⓒ after school Ⓓ inside the classroom
4. **Cathy's advice was** Ⓐ useless Ⓑ correct Ⓒ silly Ⓓ dangerous
5. **Moving the boy could have been** Ⓐ dangerous Ⓑ easy Ⓒ safe Ⓓ intelligent
6. **What did the nurse do?** Ⓐ he left the boy alone Ⓑ he sent Carlos into the school Ⓒ he put the boy's arm into a splint Ⓓ he broke the boy's arm
7. **Linda offered to** Ⓐ tell the school nurse Ⓑ find a splint Ⓒ set the arm Ⓓ help carry the boy inside
8. **What is this story mostly about?** Ⓐ a playground Ⓑ a school nurse Ⓒ a safe and wise decision Ⓓ a splint

No. right	1	2	3	4	5	6	7	8
G score	2.4	2.6	3.0	3.4	3.7	4.0	4.4	4.9

Sometimes a dog's life is not too bad. Consider Spike. He was a stray puppy. No one wanted him. He was picked up and put into a dog pound. A dog trainer saw him and liked his big feet. So Spike found a friend who taught him to growl, fight, and crawl when told to do so. Walt Disney used him in the motion picture *Old Yeller.* The stray puppy that no one wanted became a famous movie star and rode to work in an automobile. He became a million-dollar mutt.

Then there is Tinkle. This cocker spaniel has a right to be cocky. Her master is a jet pilot who has flown more than 5000 hours. Tinkle has been in the cockpit of the jet on many of these flights. She has flown a total of 3000 hours. If her owner ever flies into outer space, Tinkle will want to go along and bark at the man in the moon!

3

1. **This story tells us a dog's life is** Ⓐ very hard   Ⓑ very gay   Ⓒ not too bad   Ⓓ unhappy
2. **When a dog trainer saw a stray puppy, he liked his** Ⓐ floppy ears   Ⓑ big feet   Ⓒ long tail   Ⓓ furry coat
3. **The stray puppy was called** Ⓐ Spike   Ⓑ Mike   Ⓒ Ike   Ⓓ Stripe
4. **Tinkle is a** Ⓐ Boston terrier   Ⓑ cocker spaniel   Ⓒ fox terrier   Ⓓ great Dane
5. **Tinkle has flown how long?** Ⓐ 1000 weeks   Ⓑ 3000 days   Ⓒ 3000 hours   Ⓓ 4000 minutes
6. **What will Tinkle want to do?** Ⓐ make movies   Ⓑ crawl   Ⓒ bark at the man in the moon   Ⓓ ride in an automobile
7. **Tinkle's owner is a** Ⓐ doctor   Ⓑ movie maker   Ⓒ ship captain   Ⓓ jet pilot
8. **Spike's movie name was** Ⓐ Lassie   Ⓑ Rin Tin Tin   Ⓒ Old Yeller   Ⓓ Bullet

No. right	1	2	3	4	5	6	7	8
G score	2.9	3.3	3.5	3.7	4.0	4.3	4.6	5.0

4

Jane had made Little League! She could not believe it when the coach from the Pirates called her and told her she had been chosen for his team. She was the only girl on the Pirates team, although she wasn't the only girl in Little League.

The season opened the last Saturday in April. The Pirates played the Orioles, and the Pirates won.

Jane played outfield in the second inning. A fly ball came towards her, but she wasn't paying attention and missed it. "Wake up!" the coach yelled at her. Jane was very embarrassed. However she made up for it in the fourth inning. She was up at bat and hit a double. Two runners came home. The team and all the people sitting in the bleachers clapped and cheered. The final score was 12 to 10. The Pirates were elated. They felt they had made a good start for the season.

1. **Which Little League team was Jane on?**   Ⓐ Giants
   Ⓑ Athletics   Ⓒ Pirates   Ⓓ Orioles
2. **How many girls were there on Jane's team?**   Ⓐ one   Ⓑ two
   Ⓒ three   Ⓓ four
3. **The season opened in the month of**   Ⓐ May   Ⓑ April
   Ⓒ June   Ⓓ March
4. **Jane played outfield in the**   Ⓐ sixth inning   Ⓑ first inning
   Ⓒ second inning   Ⓓ fourth inning
5. **When the coach yelled at her Jane was**   Ⓐ afraid
   Ⓑ embarrassed   Ⓒ shy   Ⓓ tearful
6. **In the fourth inning Jane**   Ⓐ wasn't paying attention   Ⓑ was
   struck out   Ⓒ hit a double   Ⓓ was walked to first base
7. **The spectators were**   Ⓐ sitting on the grass   Ⓑ sitting in the
   bleachers   Ⓒ standing under the trees   Ⓓ standing by the fence
8. **At the end of the game the Pirates were**   Ⓐ embarrassed
   Ⓑ unhappy   Ⓒ very happy   Ⓓ miserable

No. right	1	2	3	4	5	6	7	8
G score	2.6	2.9	3.3	3.5	3.8	4.1	4.4	4.7

Do you listen to your cat when he talks to you? Think about the different sounds your cat makes. Of course you always understand his pleasant purring sound when you pet him or feed him. But what about those high and low pitched, short and long meows he makes at other times?

There is the short, chirpy mews he seems to make only when you come home. This is his way of saying, "Hello, I am glad to see you." Then there is the high pitched demanding meow, which is repeated over and over again. Now he is yelling, "I want to eat." How about that low, deep growling sound when he is angry? Maybe he is talking tough to a big dog or someone he dislikes. Listen to your cat today. He has something to say to you!

1. **A cat will purr when you**   Ⓐ come home   Ⓑ hit him   Ⓒ ignore him   Ⓓ pet him
2. **A cat purrs when he feels**   Ⓐ angry   Ⓑ happy   Ⓒ sad   Ⓓ lonely
3. **When a cat makes short chirpy mews, he is usually saying**   Ⓐ "hello"   Ⓑ "I want to eat"   Ⓒ "go away"   Ⓓ "I want to help"
4. **A demanding meow is usually**   Ⓐ low pitched and repeated   Ⓑ low pitched but not repeated   Ⓒ high pitched and repeated   Ⓓ high pitched but not repeated
5. **A cat makes a growling sound when he is**   Ⓐ happy   Ⓑ hungry   Ⓒ miserable   Ⓓ angry
6. **When a cat sees a big dog he will usually make**   Ⓐ short chirpy sounds   Ⓑ high pitch meows   Ⓒ a purring sound   Ⓓ a low deep growl
7. **The main idea of the story is**   Ⓐ cats make nice pets   Ⓑ it is easy to train a cat   Ⓒ the sounds of a cat have different meanings   Ⓓ cats are afraid of dogs
8. **This story seems to say that cats can**   Ⓐ communicate through sounds   Ⓑ use words   Ⓒ sing   Ⓓ learn to read

No. right	1	2	3	4	5	6	7	8
G score	3.0	3.3	3.5	3.7	4.0	4.3	4.6	5.1

6

The long, strong hind legs and the long ears tell the whole bunny story. With his ears he can hear the approach of an enemy, and his strong hind legs make it possible for him to jump eight feet or more and thus escape from his enemies. The set of his ears tells how a bunny is feeling. If both lie back, he is contented. If they are standing straight up, he is listening for danger. If one is bent forward and the other backward, it means, "Now just where did that sound come from?"

1. **When a rabbit's ears lie back, he is** Ⓐ anxious Ⓑ sleepy Ⓒ contented Ⓓ hungry
2. **A rabbit's hind legs are** Ⓐ short Ⓑ straight Ⓒ broad Ⓓ strong
3. **How far can this rabbit jump?** Ⓐ five feet Ⓑ six feet Ⓒ seven feet Ⓓ eight feet
4. **What tells a bunny when an enemy is near?** Ⓐ legs Ⓑ ears Ⓒ whiskers Ⓓ mouth
5. **When a bunny is listening for danger, his ears are** Ⓐ straight back Ⓑ straight up Ⓒ forward Ⓓ one backward and one forward
6. **What helps a bunny to escape from his enemy?** Ⓐ long whiskers Ⓑ long, strong hind legs Ⓒ long, strong front legs Ⓓ straight front legs
7. **When a bunny is contented his ears are** Ⓐ straight back Ⓑ forward Ⓒ straight up Ⓓ one forward and one backward
8. **This story is about** Ⓐ dogs Ⓑ cats Ⓒ foxes Ⓓ rabbits

No. right	1	2	3	4	5	6	7	8
G score	2.6	2.8	3.3	3.6	3.8	4.2	4.6	5.0

7

In May, Mrs. Lee had a baby girl. The four Brown children, who lived next door, were excited. They wanted to give a gift. Their mother said, "Why not buy a blanket? Each of you has some money." But Jean Brown, age twelve, had a different idea.

"We have other things to give," she said. "We have skills. We have talents. I can crochet. I'd like to make a blanket."

The others liked her idea. "I'm the oldest," said Peter, who was sixteen. "I can babysit. I'd like to give her three evenings free of charge, as a gift. I'll write this on a card for her now."

"I know what I can do!" said Beth, who was eight. "I take good pictures. Mrs. Lee has no camera. I'll take pictures of the baby. I'll write this on a card, too."

Seven-year-old Hugh thought and thought. "Mrs. Lee showed me how to bake oatmeal cookies. I'll bake some for her. Maybe she won't have time to bake for a while!"

1. **How many children were in the Brown family?** Ⓐ two Ⓑ three Ⓒ four Ⓓ five
2. **Mrs. Lee was the Brown children's** Ⓐ next door neighbor Ⓑ mother Ⓒ aunt Ⓓ cousin
3. **Who was the oldest child in the Brown family?** Ⓐ Hugh Ⓑ Beth Ⓒ Jean Ⓓ Peter
4. **Jean wanted to** Ⓐ take pictures Ⓑ crochet a blanket Ⓒ babysit Ⓓ bake cookies
5. **This story tells us** Ⓐ that some good gifts aren't bought in the store Ⓑ that the children had much money Ⓒ what the baby's first name was Ⓓ whether Mrs. Lee had other children
6. **Who had taught Hugh how to bake?** Ⓐ his mother Ⓑ his sister Ⓒ his brother Ⓓ Mrs. Lee
7. **Why was Beth's idea a good one?** Ⓐ because it was cheap Ⓑ because Mrs. Lee had no camera Ⓒ because she was eight Ⓓ because she could bake
8. **What was Peter's gift?** Ⓐ oatmeal cookies Ⓑ three evenings of babysitting Ⓒ a camera Ⓓ a blanket

No. right	1	2	3	4	5	6	7	8
G score	3.3	3.5	3.7	3.9	4.3	4.6	4.8	5.2

8

Very early one morning, my father came into my room. He shook me awake.

"Come on, Karen," he said. "Get the sleep out of your eyes. I want to show you something."

I followed him downstairs. It was so early, it was still dark outside. Even the seagulls were still asleep. We drove along the sandy road to the beach and climbed out of the car. The ocean looked beautiful in the early gray light. It was full of tiny sea animals called plankton. They shone like stars as the waves hit the shore. I will never forget that dawn when the beach sparkled like a dream.

1. **Karen lives** Ⓐ in the city Ⓑ near the shore Ⓒ in the mountains Ⓓ in a one-story house
2. **Karen's father** Ⓐ told her to go to sleep Ⓑ took her swimming Ⓒ woke her up early Ⓓ brought her breakfast in bed
3. **It was so early in the morning** Ⓐ the birds were singing Ⓑ Karen was dreaming Ⓒ Karen went back to sleep Ⓓ it was still dark and quiet outside
4. **Karen and her father** Ⓐ drove to the beach Ⓑ walked to the beach Ⓒ drove into town Ⓓ went fishing
5. **When they got to the beach** Ⓐ Karen went swimming Ⓑ it was too dark to see anything Ⓒ the ocean looked beautiful Ⓓ Karen wanted to go home
6. **The ocean was full of** Ⓐ swimmers Ⓑ plankton Ⓒ stars Ⓓ seagulls
7. **Karen thought the beach looked like** Ⓐ a sparkling dream Ⓑ completely dark Ⓒ it always looked Ⓓ a big pond
8. **Karen** Ⓐ is angry at her father for waking her up Ⓑ sleeps late in the morning Ⓒ collects plankton Ⓓ remembers her trip to the shining ocean

No. right	1	2	3	4	5	6	7	8
G score	2.1	2.4	2.6	3.0	3.5	4.0	4.6	5.2

A dye factory on New Mexico Street caught fire. The flames were discovered at midnight. Engine Number One was the first to answer the call of the fire alarm. When the firemen reached the building, they put up long ladders. They fought their way through thick smoke. Where was the watchman who had been seen high up on the third floor? At last the captain found him overcome by the smoke and carried him to safety. The fire raged for five hours before it was brought under control. These brave firemen risk their lives to save the lives and property of others.

9

1. **The dye factory was on a street called**   Ⓐ New Mexico   Ⓑ New Haven   Ⓒ New York   Ⓓ Newcastle
2. **The fire was discovered at**   Ⓐ two o'clock   Ⓑ three o'clock   Ⓒ ten o'clock   Ⓓ twelve o'clock
3. **The fire alarm was first answered by Engine Number**   Ⓐ One   Ⓑ Two   Ⓒ Three   Ⓓ Four
4. **One of the biggest problems was**   Ⓐ heavy traffic   Ⓑ not enough water   Ⓒ thick smoke   Ⓓ falling wood
5. **The firemen fought the fire how many hours?**   Ⓐ one   Ⓑ three   Ⓒ five   Ⓓ seven
6. **The watchman had been seen on the**   Ⓐ first floor   Ⓑ second floor   Ⓒ third floor   Ⓓ fourth floor
7. **The watchman was overcome by the**   Ⓐ flames   Ⓑ smoke   Ⓒ poison gases   Ⓓ intense heat
8. **The lives and property of others were saved by the**   Ⓐ plumbers   Ⓑ firemen   Ⓒ carpenters   Ⓓ watchman

No. right	1	2	3	4	5	6	7	8
G score	2.3	2.5	2.8	3.3	3.7	4.3	4.7	5.4

10

When quite young, Daniel Webster did not always obey the rules at school. One day his teacher caught him breaking a rule and asked him to come forward to be punished. In that school, striking the open hand with a ruler was the punishment. Daniel's hands happened to be very dirty. On the way to the teacher's desk he wiped the palm of one hand on his pants.

"Give me your hand, sir," demanded the teacher. Out went the right hand.

The teacher looked at it a moment and said, "Daniel, if you will find another hand in this schoolroom as dirty as that, I will let you go." Instantly Daniel brought out his left hand from behind his back. "Here it is, sir," he replied.

"That will do," said the teacher, laughing. "You may go."

1. **Daniel's hands were not**   Ⓐ soiled   Ⓑ dirty   Ⓒ clean   Ⓓ stained
2. **This happened**   Ⓐ at home   Ⓑ at school   Ⓒ at church   Ⓓ on the street
3. **The punishment was**   Ⓐ being struck with a ruler   Ⓑ standing in a corner   Ⓒ washing his hands   Ⓓ staying in at recess
4. **Daniel wiped his hand**   Ⓐ on a towel   Ⓑ on a paper towel   Ⓒ on a handkerchief   Ⓓ on his pants
5. **Why was he to be punished?**   Ⓐ his hands were dirty   Ⓑ he would not go forward   Ⓒ he did not obey the rules   Ⓓ he put out his hand
6. **Where was the teacher?**   Ⓐ at his desk   Ⓑ at the blackboard   Ⓒ near the door   Ⓓ in the back of the room
7. **This story is about a boy who was**   Ⓐ sad   Ⓑ clever   Ⓒ false   Ⓓ foolish
8. **Where did he find another hand as dirty?**   Ⓐ behind his back   Ⓑ in his pocket   Ⓒ among the girls   Ⓓ among the boys

No. right	1	2	3	4	5	6	7	8
G score	2.7	3.1	3.4	3.7	4.0	4.4	4.7	5.2

On an island in New York harbor is a lady holding a torch high over her head. She is not a real live lady, but a statue. She is called the Statue of Liberty.

There are boats which are used only to take visitors to and from the island. People climb a winding stair inside the Statue of Liberty and look out over the harbor from the crown on her head. Forty persons can stand in her head at one time. She is 151 feet, 1 inch from her base to the torch.

This statue was a gift to the United States from the people of France.

1. **Visitors reach the island**   Ⓐ by train   Ⓑ by swimming   Ⓒ by boat   Ⓓ by climbing
2. **The torch is**   Ⓐ on the statue's head   Ⓑ at the top of the stairs   Ⓒ in front of the statue   Ⓓ in the hand
3. **The statue is owned by**   Ⓐ the United States   Ⓑ France   Ⓒ England   Ⓓ New York
4. **The stairs of the statue are**   Ⓐ crooked   Ⓑ fifteen feet long   Ⓒ inside the statue   Ⓓ over her head
5. **The Statue of Liberty was**   Ⓐ given to France   Ⓑ bought by the United States   Ⓒ bought by New York   Ⓓ given to the United States
6. **Inside the head there is room for**   Ⓐ one person   Ⓑ two or three people   Ⓒ forty people   Ⓓ one hundred people
7. **On the head of the statue is**   Ⓐ her hand   Ⓑ a torch   Ⓒ a crown   Ⓓ a stairway
8. **People climb to the top of the statue**   Ⓐ because the stairs wind   Ⓑ to look over the harbor   Ⓒ to see how big it is   Ⓓ to stand in her head

No. right	1	2	3	4	5	6	7	8
G score	2.5	2.8	3.3	3.6	3.9	4.4	4.8	5.3

12. A crow was sitting on a branch of a tree with a piece of cheese in his beak. A hungry fox saw this and thought of a way to get the cheese. Coming and standing under the tree, he looked up and said, "What a noble bird I see above me! His beauty is without equal. His feathers are dazzling. If only his voice is as sweet as his looks are handsome, he must be the King of the Birds." The crow heard this and just to show the fox that he could sing, he gave a loud caw. Down came the cheese, of course, and the fox snatched it up and ate it.

1. **The fox was** Ⓐ handsome   Ⓑ colorful   Ⓒ clever   Ⓓ in a tree
2. **He got the cheese by**   Ⓐ a trick   Ⓑ snatching the crow   Ⓒ climbing the tree   Ⓓ singing
3. **How did the crow feel when he heard the fox's words?**   Ⓐ flattered   Ⓑ afraid   Ⓒ sweet   Ⓓ equal
4. **The fox said that no other bird was**   Ⓐ as big   Ⓑ as good looking   Ⓒ as loud   Ⓓ as good a singer
5. **The fox said that the crow had**   Ⓐ brightly colored feathers   Ⓑ a beautiful voice   Ⓒ excellent cheese   Ⓓ intelligence
6. **A crow's voice is**   Ⓐ sweet   Ⓑ musical   Ⓒ soft   Ⓓ a harsh caw
7. **The cheese dropped when**   Ⓐ the crow opened his mouth   Ⓑ the fox opened his mouth   Ⓒ the crow fell   Ⓓ the fox cawed
8. **The crow did not have**   Ⓐ feathers   Ⓑ good sense   Ⓒ a loud voice   Ⓓ a beak

No. right	1	2	3	4	5	6	7	8
G score	3.1	3.4	3.7	3.9	4.3	4.6	5.0	5.4

Martin watched his mother making applesauce. It looked so easy that he asked to make it all by himself.

First he washed the apples and cut them in quarters. Next, after taking out the cores, he put the apples in a pan with just enough water to cover them. He cooked them until they were soft. Then he pressed them through a sieve in order to take out the skins and to make the sauce smooth. When this was finished, he put in sugar to sweeten it and then grated nutmeg over the top.

Do you think you could do what Martin did?

13

1. **This lesson tells how to make apple** Ⓐ tarts Ⓑ pie Ⓒ sauce Ⓓ cake
2. **The apples were first** Ⓐ peeled Ⓑ washed Ⓒ grated Ⓓ sweetened
3. **Martin cut each of the apples into** Ⓐ two parts Ⓑ three parts Ⓒ four parts Ⓓ five parts
4. **Enough water was used to** Ⓐ cover the bottom of the pan Ⓑ fill the pan Ⓒ cover all the apples Ⓓ cover part of the apples
5. **The apples were cooked** Ⓐ one hour Ⓑ until they were soft Ⓒ until they boiled Ⓓ ten minutes
6. **To sweeten the apples Martin put in** Ⓐ maple syrup Ⓑ molasses Ⓒ honey Ⓓ sugar
7. **The flavoring was** Ⓐ salt Ⓑ lemon Ⓒ chocolate Ⓓ nutmeg
8. **This story happened in the** Ⓐ bedroom Ⓑ kitchen Ⓒ living room Ⓓ dining room

No. right	1	2	3	4	5	6	7	8
G score	2.2	2.4	2.7	3.3	3.7	4.2	4.7	5.4

14

Abby's father died suddenly when she was thirteen. At first, all the adults were so upset, Abby thought she shouldn't cry. Then, her younger brothers and sisters cried all the time, so she thought she should take care of them. She didn't cry for a long time. She thought her father would come back. She listened for him in the morning, and at night when he used to come and tuck her into bed. One day, Abby woke up and began to cry. She cried and cried, and when she stopped, she knew her father was dead. She stopped listening for him and began to miss him.

1. **When Abby was thirteen**   Ⓐ her father went away   Ⓑ she left home   Ⓒ her father died   Ⓓ her family moved
2. **At first, Abby**   Ⓐ cried and cried   Ⓑ took care of the adults   Ⓒ talked to her friends   Ⓓ didn't cry
3. **Abby thought she should**   Ⓐ be upset   Ⓑ take care of her brothers and sisters   Ⓒ cry all the time   Ⓓ leave everyone alone
4. **For a long time, Abby thought**   Ⓐ her brothers and sisters were listening   Ⓑ her mother was upset   Ⓒ her father would come back   Ⓓ she was all alone
5. **She listened for her father**   Ⓐ to come home from work   Ⓑ to sing to her   Ⓒ to laugh with her   Ⓓ to tuck her into bed
6. **One day, Abby woke up and**   Ⓐ began to cry   Ⓑ saw her father again   Ⓒ listened   Ⓓ forgot her father
7. **This story is mainly about**   Ⓐ listening and waiting   Ⓑ Abby and her brothers and sisters   Ⓒ Abby and the death of her father   Ⓓ crying children
8. **Abby knew her father was dead when**   Ⓐ she was told   Ⓑ the adults were upset   Ⓒ the children cried   Ⓓ she stopped crying

No. right	1	2	3	4	5	6	7	8
G score	2.5	2.8	3.3	3.7	4.0	4.5	5.0	5.5

Rosa was given a bicycle for her birthday. She thought it was beautiful.

When her father had come home from work on Friday, they went out to buy it. Rosa had often walked round the bicycle shop and knew there was a red one in the middle of the showroom. That was the one she wanted. The chrome was like silver and there was black tape round the handle bars. It had a reflector on the back wheel and a big lamp in front.

The salesman put the bicycle in the trunk of the car. They drove home. As the next day was her birthday, Rosa's father had given her the bicycle right away.

1. **Rosa thought the bicycle was** Ⓐ ordinary Ⓑ pretty Ⓒ beautiful Ⓓ handsome
2. **Rosa and her father went shopping** Ⓐ before her father went to work Ⓑ when her father came home from work Ⓒ on Friday morning Ⓓ after dinner
3. **The bicycle Rosa wanted was** Ⓐ in the shop window Ⓑ outside the shop Ⓒ in the showroom Ⓓ on a rack
4. **The bicycle was** Ⓐ silver Ⓑ gold Ⓒ red Ⓓ black
5. **On the back wheel there was** Ⓐ tape Ⓑ a reflector Ⓒ a lamp Ⓓ a mirror
6. **Who put the bicycle in the car?** Ⓐ the salesman Ⓑ Rosa's father Ⓒ Rosa and her father Ⓓ the salesman and Rosa's father
7. **Rosa's birthday was on** Ⓐ Thursday Ⓑ Friday Ⓒ Saturday Ⓓ Sunday
8. **Rosa was given the bicycle** Ⓐ the next day Ⓑ after dinner Ⓒ on Sunday Ⓓ when they got home

No. right	1	2	3	4	5	6	7	8
G score	2.5	2.8	3.3	3.7	4.0	4.5	5.0	5.5

16

There is a water spider who lives under water. She breathes the air in little bubbles held close to her body. She will soon have baby spiders.

She finds a place among the leaves of some underwater plant, or perhaps in a drowned log, that would make a good little nest. She spins the silky walls and ceiling of a web house, closed at the top and open at the bottom, like a bell. But it is full of water!

She finds a large air bubble at the surface of the water. She carries it down to the nest, and she leaves it there. She swims up again and gets another bubble of air, and brings it down. She does this again and again till the bubbles push all the water out of the nest. Now there is enough air for her and her babies to live in before the little ones are old enough to swim.

1. **This lesson is mainly about** Ⓐ spiders Ⓑ learning to swim Ⓒ breathing under water Ⓓ a water spider
2. **What is the first thing the spider does?** Ⓐ finds her babies Ⓑ finds a place for a nest Ⓒ blows a bubble Ⓓ spins a web
3. **Why do the bubbles in the nest not float up and away?** Ⓐ the ceiling stops them Ⓑ the spider holds them down Ⓒ the babies cling to them Ⓓ they are heavier than water
4. **What word describes the nest?** Ⓐ dry Ⓑ silky Ⓒ round Ⓓ closed
5. **Where does the spider bring air bubbles?** Ⓐ to the bottom of the nest Ⓑ to her little ones Ⓒ to fish Ⓓ to a window in the nest
6. **Where is the spider's nest?** Ⓐ in a corner Ⓑ in a bell Ⓒ in the leaves of a tree Ⓓ under water
7. **What is drowned in the story?** Ⓐ a spider Ⓑ a log Ⓒ baby spiders Ⓓ fish
8. **The spiders need air** Ⓐ to swim Ⓑ to breathe Ⓒ to spin Ⓓ to grow leaves

No. right	1	2	3	4	5	6	7	8
G score	3.2	3.4	3.7	4.0	4.3	4.6	5.1	5.5

It's a special day at the stadium. This special day is called "Family Day." A little later, there will be a major baseball game between two teams of the National League. But first is another kind of baseball game. This time, the players are the children of the stars!

Ten-year-old Lisa comes up to bat. Great swing, Lisa! She hits it on the first pitch and runs safely to second base.

John, who is nine, is a good batter, too. Brian, age five, strikes out. He'll be better when he's older. Then Jennifer comes up to the plate. She is eight. Strike one. Strike two. Then a hit. Jennifer is making a home run.

All the children may play. It's Scott's turn now. Scott is only two. He misses the ball but he starts to walk the bases. Why not? "That's where the big kids go," he says to himself. "Make the rules fair for a little guy like me." He passes first base. He passes second base. He toddles farther and farther. But now he is way into the outfield. Daddy jumps up and runs out to get him. All the spectators are laughing.

17

1. **This story is about** Ⓐ football Ⓑ soccer Ⓒ baseball Ⓓ basketball
2. **Who is the first child up to bat?** Ⓐ Scott Ⓑ Lisa Ⓒ Brian Ⓓ Jennifer
3. **Who makes the home run?** Ⓐ Scott Ⓑ Lisa Ⓒ Brian Ⓓ Jennifer
4. **Scott toddles** Ⓐ into the outfield Ⓑ to third base Ⓒ to the home plate Ⓓ to the bench
5. **Who is the youngest player?** Ⓐ John Ⓑ Brian Ⓒ Scott Ⓓ Lisa
6. **What does Brian do?** Ⓐ makes it to second Ⓑ strikes out Ⓒ makes a home run Ⓓ runs to the outfield
7. **This day is called** Ⓐ Children's Day Ⓑ Major League Day Ⓒ Parents' Day Ⓓ Family Day
8. **In the first game, the players are** Ⓐ the children of baseball stars Ⓑ the spectators Ⓒ the baseball stars Ⓓ the whole family

No. right	1	2	3	4	5	6	7	8
G score	2.5	2.8	3.3	3.6	4.0	4.4	4.9	5.5

18

Have you ever noticed how people are like their dogs? My grandmother has soft, curly, white hair, and sleepy-looking eyes. Her dog, Prince, has soft, curly hair too. He spends the day on the floor asleep. The boy who lives next door plays a lot of sports. He has long legs and cannot sit still. He owns a racing dog. They go jogging together. And the day before Mrs. Rice had her baby, guess what? Winnie, her dog, had a litter of puppies. Maybe dogs want to be like us. I'll have to go ask Monster, my St. Bernard, what he thinks.

1. **The author thinks** Ⓐ people aren't nice to their dogs Ⓑ dogs act like their owners Ⓒ dogs are bad pets Ⓓ it's hard to take care of a dog

2. **The grandmother** Ⓐ is too old to have a dog Ⓑ calls her dog Curley Ⓒ has a dog that sleeps a lot Ⓓ likes cats better

3. **The boy next door** Ⓐ is lazy Ⓑ sleeps too much Ⓒ doesn't like his pet Ⓓ plays a lot of sports

4. **His dog** Ⓐ plays sports Ⓑ goes jogging with him Ⓒ chases cars Ⓓ had puppies

5. **Mrs. Rice's dog's name is** Ⓐ Winnie Ⓑ Prince Ⓒ St. Bernard Ⓓ Monster

6. **Winnie and Mrs. Rice** Ⓐ go running together Ⓑ fight with each other Ⓒ are both mothers Ⓓ live in different homes

7. **The author's grandmother probably** Ⓐ eats a lot Ⓑ rests a lot Ⓒ plays sports Ⓓ jogs

8. **If the author is right, and people are like their dogs, the author** Ⓐ is big Ⓑ is sleepy Ⓒ races Ⓓ is a mother

No. right	1	2	3	4	5	6	7	8
G score	2.8	3.3	3.6	3.8	4.3	4.7	5.2	5.6

Your heart is made of muscle and is only about the size of a fist. It works like a pump to send blood to all parts of your body. But what makes it beat?

The sound of the heartbeat is caused by the closing of the valves in your heart. These valves open and close to keep all the blood flowing in the right direction. When they close, they go "thump." But what makes the valves open and close?

There is a small strip of tissue in the heart called the pacemaker. This sends out an electrical impulse and automatically keeps your heart beating. If this pacemaker wears out, doctors can replace it with one that is artificial.

19

1. **Your heart works**   Ⓐ very hard   Ⓑ like a pump   Ⓒ better with an artificial pacemaker   Ⓓ on electricity
2. **Your heart is about the size of a**   Ⓐ valve   Ⓑ pump   Ⓒ fist   Ⓓ muscle
3. **The beating of the heart is the sound of**   Ⓐ the valves closing   Ⓑ the blood flowing   Ⓒ an electrical impulse   Ⓓ a pacemaker
4. **Blood is pumped**   Ⓐ to your muscles   Ⓑ to all parts of your body   Ⓒ to your fists   Ⓓ only by the tissues
5. **Heart valves open and close**   Ⓐ to make your heart beat   Ⓑ about nine times a minute   Ⓒ to keep the heart muscles strong   Ⓓ to keep the blood flowing in the right direction
6. **The small strip of tissue is called**   Ⓐ the heart   Ⓑ the pacemaker   Ⓒ the peacemaker   Ⓓ artificial
7. **The small strip of tissue sends out**   Ⓐ blood   Ⓑ heartbeats   Ⓒ an electrical impulse   Ⓓ "thumps"
8. **If a pacemaker wears out, doctors can**   Ⓐ give you a new heart   Ⓑ replace it   Ⓒ do nothing   Ⓓ close the valves

No. right	1	2	3	4	5	6	7	8
G score	2.7	3.2	3.5	3.8	4.3	4.7	5.3	5.8

20

One summer Ruth and her father and mother visited her aunt in Venice, Italy. They stayed in her aunt's house near the sea. One day Ruth's aunt took her guests sight-seeing. Ruth was surprised to find that canals were used instead of streets. The water in the canals flowed in from the sea. That day she saw no horses, carriages, or cars. People went about in boats just as we ride in cars. The children of Venice might be surprised to ride in our automobiles and buses, just as Ruth was surprised at having a boat ride.

1. **Who took Ruth sight-seeing? Her** Ⓐ uncle Ⓑ cousin Ⓒ aunt Ⓓ mother
2. **Ruth found that the streets were** Ⓐ wooden blocks Ⓑ canals Ⓒ paved roads Ⓓ dirt roads
3. **People of Venice went about in** Ⓐ carts Ⓑ boats Ⓒ buses Ⓓ automobiles
4. **Ruth went to Venice in the** Ⓐ autumn Ⓑ summer Ⓒ spring Ⓓ winter
5. **Her aunt's house was** Ⓐ on a mountain Ⓑ by the side of a river Ⓒ near the sea Ⓓ next to the church
6. **How many horses, carriages, and cars did she see?** Ⓐ none Ⓑ a few Ⓒ several Ⓓ many
7. **The water of the canals flowed in from the** Ⓐ sea Ⓑ rivers Ⓒ lakes Ⓓ ponds
8. **What is this story mainly about?** Ⓐ Ruth's visit to the seashore Ⓑ Ruth's visit to a strange city Ⓒ a girl who took a ride in a rowboat Ⓓ a spring vacation

Dolly was a very smart dog. She had two pups that she loved very much. Sometimes her owner was good to the three dogs, but often he came home angry. Then he kicked Dolly and the pups until they cried.

One day when the owner was away from home, the neighbors saw Dolly going down the street carrying a pup by the nape of its neck. After a time she came back and carried the other pup down the street.

A curious neighbor followed to see what she was doing with her pups. Each one had been placed on the doorstep of a different home. These people had always been kind to Dolly when they visited her owner. Finally, Dolly returned to her own home to bear alone the kicks of her cruel owner for the rest of her life.

21

1. **This is the story of a dog's** Ⓐ owner Ⓑ hatred Ⓒ fear for herself Ⓓ love for her pups
2. **Dolly had how many pups?** Ⓐ four Ⓑ three Ⓒ two Ⓓ one
3. **When Dolly carried her pups away, her owner was** Ⓐ sleeping Ⓑ not at home Ⓒ eating Ⓓ gardening
4. **Dolly was** Ⓐ pretty Ⓑ smart Ⓒ cruel Ⓓ dull
5. **Dolly was taking each of her pups to** Ⓐ a new home Ⓑ the dog pound Ⓒ the police station Ⓓ the railroad station
6. **Dolly carried her pups by** Ⓐ their front legs Ⓑ their tails Ⓒ their back legs Ⓓ the napes of their necks
7. **Who followed Dolly?** Ⓐ a policeman Ⓑ the milkman Ⓒ a neighbor Ⓓ her owner
8. **The people to whom Dolly took her pups were** Ⓐ mean Ⓑ kind Ⓒ poor Ⓓ blind

No. right	1	2	3	4	5	6	7	8
G score	3.2	3.5	3.8	4.2	4.6	5.0	5.4	5.8

22

"If only I could star in one sport!" So many of us say that to ourselves. Jim Thorpe starred in more than one and has gone down in history as a great all-around athlete.

He was born in Oklahoma in 1886. As an American Indian, he lived on a reservation. His father wanted him to have a good education. He sent Jim away to a boarding school for Indians. Jim didn't like being away from his family, but he learned to play football at that school.

In 1912 Jim Thorpe was an Olympic winner in track and field. As an adult he became a famous football star. At that time he was already playing major league baseball.

1. **Jim went to a school for** Ⓐ American Indians Ⓑ sport stars Ⓒ orphans Ⓓ reservations
2. **Jim's father sent him away to school** Ⓐ to learn to play football Ⓑ to get a good education Ⓒ to learn history Ⓓ because he was bored away from his family
3. **At school Jim learned to play** Ⓐ baseball Ⓑ football Ⓒ basketball Ⓓ volleyball
4. **When he was at school, Jim felt** Ⓐ like a star Ⓑ homesick Ⓒ reserved Ⓓ important in history
5. **Jim Thorpe was an Olympic winner in** Ⓐ football Ⓑ baseball Ⓒ track and field Ⓓ all sports
6. **In baseball Jim played** Ⓐ major league Ⓑ minor league Ⓒ little league Ⓓ international league
7. **Jim starred in all but** Ⓐ track and field Ⓑ baseball Ⓒ football Ⓓ field hockey
8. **This story is mainly about** Ⓐ a boarding school Ⓑ an all-around athlete Ⓒ an Indian reservation Ⓓ Oklahoma

No. right	1	2	3	4	5	6	7	8
G score	2.7	3.1	3.5	3.8	4.3	4.7	5.3	5.8

Heidi had broken her leg, but the cast was off now. The little dog was not sure at first that she was better. One day the vet said, "It's entirely healed." Heidi seemed to forget her injury and ran gaily as she'd done before.

We were surprised to see her begin to limp again. Had something gone wrong? When I was too busy to play with her, or if I said no to an extra cookie, she limped.

One day my cousins came to visit. We all sat in the yard. Little Alfredo was afraid of dogs, so we kept Heidi inside the house.

Heidi was unhappy there. Later we noticed her limping again. Now we knew.

"Oh, Heidi!" I cried. "You're not fooling us anymore! You want us to feel sorry for you!" I shook my head. "You're just like a human!"

1. **Heidi was**   Ⓐ a little girl   Ⓑ a little cat   Ⓒ a little dog   Ⓓ a vet
2. **When my cousins came to visit, we sat**   Ⓐ in the kitchen   Ⓑ in the yard   Ⓒ in the bedroom   Ⓓ on the porch
3. **Little Alfredo**   Ⓐ was afraid of dogs   Ⓑ was afraid of cats   Ⓒ loved dogs   Ⓓ loved cats
4. **When Heidi wanted something, she**   Ⓐ barked   Ⓑ whined   Ⓒ did tricks   Ⓓ limped
5. **The vet said the leg was**   Ⓐ still broken   Ⓑ getting worse   Ⓒ entirely healed   Ⓓ getting better
6. **When Heidi limped, she thought people would**   Ⓐ feel sorry for her   Ⓑ bring her to the vet   Ⓒ be angry   Ⓓ be afraid
7. **Inside the house, Heidi was**   Ⓐ afraid   Ⓑ busy   Ⓒ playful   Ⓓ unhappy
8. **This story is mainly about**   Ⓐ a visit from cousins   Ⓑ a dog who limped when she wanted something   Ⓒ how Heidi broke her leg   Ⓓ a visit to the vet

No. right	1	2	3	4	5	6	7	8
G score	2.7	3.2	3.6	3.9	4.4	4.8	5.3	5.9

24

Let me tell you about the lamplighter. At dusk he came riding up our street on his bicycle. It was an old black bicycle without gears. All the year round he wore a brown raincoat and plaid cap. In his hand he held a wooden pole, about six feet long. His job was to turn on the streetlights one by one.

Our street was on a slight hill. Beginning at the bottom, the lamplighter rode his bicycle to the first lamp. Never stopping, he used the pole held high above his head to push a switch. He never missed. Then he rode on to the next streetlight. This was across the street, not opposite the first one, but a little further up. And so the lamplighter rode, weaving his way from one side of our street to the other, filling it with little pools of light.

1. **The lamplighter came at**　Ⓐ evening　Ⓑ dawn　Ⓒ mid-day　Ⓓ midnight
2. **The lamplighter's bicycle was**　Ⓐ brown　Ⓑ black　Ⓒ green　Ⓓ white
3. **The lamplighter always wore**　Ⓐ a jacket　Ⓑ a raincoat　Ⓒ overalls　Ⓓ a uniform
4. **How long was the wooden pole?**　Ⓐ four feet　Ⓑ seven feet　Ⓒ six feet　Ⓓ sixty feet
5. **The street was**　Ⓐ curved　Ⓑ straight　Ⓒ a hill　Ⓓ a dead end
6. **To light the street lights the lamplighter**　Ⓐ stopped riding but didn't get off his bicycle　Ⓑ got off his bicycle　Ⓒ went on riding　Ⓓ walked up the street
7. **The next light was**　Ⓐ opposite the first one　Ⓑ on the same side of the street　Ⓒ on the other side of the street, but not opposite　Ⓓ in the middle of the street
8. **Choose the best title:**　Ⓐ In the Old Days　Ⓑ The Lamplighter　Ⓒ Bicycle Riding　Ⓓ The First Electric Street Lights

No. right	1	2	3	4	5	6	7	8
G score	2.7	3.2	3.5	3.8	4.3	4.7	5.3	5.8

Curly is my big black dog. He is so strong that he can carry me on his back. He likes to run and play with me. He likes to follow my father around in the fields too. One day my father took off his coat and laid it on the ground under a big oak tree. Curly stood watching him. My father said, "Watch my coat, Curly."

Curly sat down on the coat. My father forgot all about his coat and went home without it. Late in the evening I missed my dog. I looked everywhere for him, calling, "Curly, Curly!" But Curly did not come. Soon my father wanted something that was in his coat pocket. Then he remembered what he had done. He went back to the big oak tree. What do you think he saw? Curly was sitting on the coat so that nobody could carry it away.

25

1. **Curly is a** Ⓐ boy Ⓑ man Ⓒ tree Ⓓ dog
2. **The dog is** Ⓐ brown Ⓑ white Ⓒ black Ⓓ yellow
3. **Curly took care of the** Ⓐ man Ⓑ coat Ⓒ watch Ⓓ tree
4. **When did we miss the dog?** Ⓐ in the morning Ⓑ at noon Ⓒ at 4 o'clock Ⓓ in the evening
5. **The dog did not come when he was called because he was** Ⓐ on guard Ⓑ afraid Ⓒ asleep Ⓓ not hungry
6. **My father placed the coat** Ⓐ in the oak tree Ⓑ on the ground Ⓒ in the garden Ⓓ over Curly
7. **This story was written to tell about** Ⓐ an obedient dog Ⓑ a forgetful farmer Ⓒ a little boy Ⓓ a man's coat
8. **Which statement is false?** Ⓐ Curly was faithful to his master. Ⓑ Curly liked to play. Ⓒ Curly was strong. Ⓓ Curly was mischievous.

No. right	1	2	3	4	5	6	7	8
G score	1.7	2.0	2.4	2.8	3.6	4.3	5.1	6.0

26

A lion was asleep in his den. A mouse ran across his face and woke him up. The lion lost his temper, caught the mouse with his paw, and was about to kill him. The mouse was terrified and begged the lion to spare his life. "Please let me go," he cried, "and one day I will repay you for your kindness." The idea of so tiny a creature ever being able to do anything for him made the lion laugh aloud, and he let the mouse go.

But the mouse's chance came after all. One day the lion got tangled in a net that had been spread by some hunters. The lion roared in anger, and the mouse heard him. He ran to the spot and set to work. He gnawed the ropes with his teeth and, before long, set the lion free. "There," said the mouse. "You laughed at me when I promised that I would repay you. Now you see that even a little mouse can help a big lion."

1. **How did the lion feel when the mouse woke him up?** Ⓐ angry Ⓑ kind Ⓒ free Ⓓ terrified
2. **The lion** Ⓐ killed the mouse Ⓑ seized the mouse Ⓒ woke the mouse up Ⓓ repayed the mouse
3. **The mouse was** Ⓐ laughing Ⓑ very frightened Ⓒ roaring Ⓓ tangled
4. **What did the mouse promise the lion?** Ⓐ to pay him Ⓑ to return the favor Ⓒ to be kind Ⓓ never to wake him up again
5. **The lion thought the idea of a mouse helping him was** Ⓐ amusing Ⓑ a trick Ⓒ possible Ⓓ clever
6. **One day the lion** Ⓐ got tangled in his den Ⓑ was shot by hunters Ⓒ became trapped Ⓓ spread a net
7. **What did the mouse do?** Ⓐ he chewed through the net Ⓑ he gnawed the lion's paw Ⓒ he roared in anger Ⓓ he begged the hunters to set the lion free
8. **What lesson can be learned from this story?** Ⓐ it is wrong to hunt animals Ⓑ mice should not be afraid of lions Ⓒ small creatures can sometimes help big ones Ⓓ never break a promise

No. right	1	2	3	4	5	6	7	8
G score	2.5	2.8	3.3	3.7	4.3	4.7	5.4	6.0

Alex was a musician. He played the flute in an orchestra. He gave music lessons every day. When there was a parade, he marched with the band. Even when Alex wasn't playing the flute, he heard music everywhere. The noise of the trucks in the street seemed like the roll of drums to him. His squeaky apartment door sounded like a violin. And at night, when his cat sat on his lap, her purr was like a very, very soft bell. Nothing Alex heard was just a noise to him. It was all music. It was as if an orchestra played just for him, wherever he went.

1. **Alex was**   Ⓐ a dancer   Ⓑ a cat   Ⓒ in a circus   Ⓓ a musician
2. **His instrument was the**   Ⓐ trumpet   Ⓑ drum   Ⓒ flute   Ⓓ violin
3. **Every day, Alex**   Ⓐ marched with a parade   Ⓑ gave flute lessons   Ⓒ rode a bus   Ⓓ watched a play
4. **Alex was different from other people because**   Ⓐ he had a cat   Ⓑ he lived in an apartment   Ⓒ he heard music wherever he went   Ⓓ he liked music
5. **The sound of his apartment door squeaking made Alex think of**   Ⓐ a violin   Ⓑ his cat   Ⓒ getting it fixed   Ⓓ a bell
6. **At night, Alex's cat**   Ⓐ played in an orchestra   Ⓑ sat in his lap   Ⓒ ate her dinner   Ⓓ was lonely
7. **What we would call noise, Alex would call**   Ⓐ music   Ⓑ sounds   Ⓒ silence   Ⓓ funny
8. **Choose the best title:**   Ⓐ The Orchestra   Ⓑ City Noise   Ⓒ Alex's Musical World   Ⓓ Playing in a Marching Band

No. right	1	2	3	4	5	6	7	8
G score	1.8	2.3	2.6	3.2	3.7	4.4	5.3	6.0

28

Every June, Douglas went on a picnic with his grandparents. This year Douglas asked his grandmother if he could bring Juan with him. Juan had recently moved to the neighborhood. Douglas wanted to show Juan his favorite picnic place.

They went on a Sunday. It was a cool day, and there were lots of clouds in the sky. It looked as if it could rain, but Douglas didn't mind. He knew they'd have a good time.

While his grandfather cooked the hamburgers, Douglas and Juan played wiffle ball. After lunch they all walked through the woods to the stream. Douglas and Juan took off their sneakers and socks and put their feet in the water. Juan caught a crayfish. Douglas tried to catch a frog, but it was too quick for him and got away.

---

1. **When Douglas wanted to bring Juan he asked his**
   Ⓐ grandparents   Ⓑ grandfather   Ⓒ grandmother   Ⓓ mother
2. **Juan was**   Ⓐ a visitor   Ⓑ staying with Douglas
   Ⓒ a neighbor   Ⓓ an old friend
3. **The day was**   Ⓐ sunny   Ⓑ hot   Ⓒ rainy   Ⓓ cloudy
4. **Grandfather cooked**   Ⓐ chicken   Ⓑ steak   Ⓒ hamburger
   Ⓓ hot dogs
5. **Douglas and Juan played**   Ⓐ baseball   Ⓑ softball   Ⓒ wiffle
   ball   Ⓓ volley ball
6. **To reach the stream they walked**   Ⓐ across a field   Ⓑ through
   the woods   Ⓒ over a bridge   Ⓓ down the road
7. **Juan caught**   Ⓐ a frog   Ⓑ a crayfish   Ⓒ a minnow
   Ⓓ a tadpole
8. **Juan and Douglas were wearing**   Ⓐ shoes   Ⓑ sandals
   Ⓒ sneakers   Ⓓ cleats

No. right	1	2	3	4	5	6	7	8
G score	2.6	3.0	3.5	3.8	4.3	4.8	5.4	6.0

I know a man who loves hats. The walls of his house are covered with hats of every size, shape, and style you can imagine. He has army hats from every war of the last two centuries. He has formal top hats once worn by men who rode to the opera in horse-drawn carriages. He has a miner's hat with a bright light on its crown. He has tall white chef's hats and short white surgeon's caps. He has a ten-gallon hat hanging next to an Indian chief's grand, eagle-feathered headdress. Is it any wonder that I call my friend The Mad Hatter?

29

1. **The author** Ⓐ loves hats Ⓑ has a friend who loves hats Ⓒ never wears a hat Ⓓ collects hats
2. **The man's walls are** Ⓐ covered with wallpaper Ⓑ brightly painted Ⓒ hung with a lot of hats Ⓓ full of paintings
3. **His army hat collection** Ⓐ has 200 hats Ⓑ is famous Ⓒ belongs to a museum Ⓓ has hats from a lot of wars
4. **His formal top hats were worn by** Ⓐ actors on stage Ⓑ famous kings Ⓒ men who once went to the opera Ⓓ magicians
5. **A miner's hat has a light on it because** Ⓐ it lights his way in the dark mines Ⓑ it's easier to find the hat Ⓒ it's more stylish Ⓓ it keeps his head warm
6. **The chef's hat and the surgeon's cap** Ⓐ are the same shape Ⓑ hang next to each other Ⓒ are both white Ⓓ are the same size
7. **The cowboy's hat hangs next to** Ⓐ the surgeon's cap Ⓑ the Indian chief's headdress Ⓒ the eagle Ⓓ the army hats
8. **The author calls the man** Ⓐ The Cat in the Hat Ⓑ The Hat Man Ⓒ The Hat Rack Ⓓ The Mad Hatter

No. right	1	2	3	4	5	6	7	8
G score	2.8	3.3	3.6	4.0	4.5	5.0	5.5	6.0

30

The customs of people in other countries may appear strange to us. And some of our ways must seem just as strange to them. For example, let us look at some old Japanese customs.

We sleep on soft pillows and beds; they sleep on hard ones. We wash our faces and wipe them dry with towels; they wipe their faces with wet towels. We lower our faces when we say prayers; they raise theirs. When entering houses, our men take off their hats; the Japanese take off their shoes. We give gifts when arriving; they leave them when departing. We open gifts in front of the giver; they never do. When in mourning, we wear black; they wear white. We frown when scolded; they smile.

When we say that the customs of people in other countries are strange, they could reply, "The same to you!"

1. **The main idea of this lesson is** Ⓐ there is only one right way to do everything Ⓑ each nation believes that the customs of other nations are strange Ⓒ American habits are better than Japanese habits Ⓓ Japanese ways are better than American ways
2. **The pillows Japanese sleep on are** Ⓐ firm Ⓑ soft Ⓒ fluffy Ⓓ springy
3. **The towels with which Japanese wipe their faces are** Ⓐ dry Ⓑ damp Ⓒ warm Ⓓ wet
4. **During mourning, what color is worn by the Japanese?** Ⓐ gray Ⓑ white Ⓒ black Ⓓ pale blue
5. **Japanese guests present their gifts** Ⓐ upon arrival Ⓑ while visiting Ⓒ at departure Ⓓ after departure
6. **When saying prayers, the Japanese** Ⓐ lower their faces Ⓑ raise their faces Ⓒ smile Ⓓ close their eyes
7. **When Japanese children are scolded, they** Ⓐ cry Ⓑ frown Ⓒ pout Ⓓ smile
8. **The Japanese probably think our behavior is** Ⓐ wrong Ⓑ strange Ⓒ right Ⓓ uncivilized

No. right	1	2	3	4	5	6	7	8
G score	3.2	3.5	3.8	4.3	4.6	5.1	5.6	6.0

The young teacher, Miss Tyler, played the guitar. One day she led her class in singing "He's Got the Whole World in His Hands."

There were thirty children in this class. There was no time to sing each child's name separately, so she would pick two at a time. They would sing, for instance "He's got John and Victor in His hands." She always called out two boys or two girls.

Soon only Alberto and Karen were left. So she sang their names together. Alberto and Karen made a face.

"Is there anyone we missed?" Miss Tyler asked.

"Yes!" the children cried. "Miss Tyler and Mr. Benson!" Mr. Benson was the handsome young teacher next door.

Miss Tyler turned red. "Oh, let's take the names separately this time."

"Oh, no!" the children laughed. "Fair is fair! You did it to us!"

1. **Miss Tyler played the** Ⓐ piano Ⓑ flute Ⓒ drums Ⓓ guitar
2. **How many children were in the class?** Ⓐ ten Ⓑ twenty Ⓒ thirty Ⓓ forty
3. **Mr. Benson was a** Ⓐ teacher Ⓑ parent Ⓒ principal Ⓓ singer
4. **Who made a face?** Ⓐ John and Victor Ⓑ Alberto and Karen Ⓒ Miss Tyler Ⓓ Mr. Benson
5. **The children were** Ⓐ singing Ⓑ reading Ⓒ writing Ⓓ drawing
6. **When the children cried, "Miss Tyler and Mr. Benson!", Miss Tyler** Ⓐ was happy Ⓑ said yes Ⓒ blushed Ⓓ called Mr. Benson
7. **The children probably thought that** Ⓐ Miss Tyler couldn't sing Ⓑ Alberto liked Karen very much Ⓒ Mr. Benson was ugly Ⓓ Miss Tyler liked Mr. Benson very much.
8. **The class was singing** Ⓐ one name at a time Ⓑ two names at a time Ⓒ three names at a time Ⓓ four names at a time

No. right	1	2	3	4	5	6	7	8
G score	2.0	2.4	2.8	3.5	4.3	5.1	6.0	7.0

32

John woke up very early. It was Christmas morning. He sat up quickly and felt towards the foot of his bed. Last night he'd put his stocking there. It was a big, green knitted stocking which his grandmother had made. He found it in the dark. It was full of interesting shapes now. At the toe he felt something round and smooth. Above that, his fingers found a hard square shape.

John longed to open the presents in his stocking. He put on his flashlight and carefully pulled out a long heavy package. It was wrapped in red tissue paper. He tore off the paper. Inside was a hammer. He had wanted a hammer more than anything else in the world. He went on opening the little packages. There was scotch tape, batteries, a box of nails, candy, and, in the toe, an orange. John was very happy. He lay down again with all his presents around him. As he fell asleep, he heard the grandfather clock in the hall strike three.

1. **When John woke up he was**   Ⓐ happy   Ⓑ unhappy
   Ⓒ excited   Ⓓ tired
2. **What color was John's stocking?**   Ⓐ red   Ⓑ yellow
   Ⓒ green   Ⓓ orange
3. **To open his presents John**   Ⓐ put on the light   Ⓑ put on his flashlight   Ⓒ opened the door   Ⓓ pulled up the shade
4. **The first gift he opened was wrapped in**   Ⓐ shiny paper
   Ⓑ tissue paper   Ⓒ newspaper   Ⓓ birthday paper
5. **John's favorite present was**   Ⓐ a chisel   Ⓑ a screwdriver
   Ⓒ a hammer   Ⓓ a fishing rod
6. **John heard the clock strike**   Ⓐ five o'clock   Ⓑ four o'clock
   Ⓒ six o'clock   Ⓓ three o'clock
7. **In the toe John found**   Ⓐ an apple   Ⓑ an orange   Ⓒ candy
   Ⓓ a tennis ball
8. **It is implied in the story that John's hobby is**   Ⓐ painting
   Ⓑ building   Ⓒ fishing   Ⓓ swimming

No. right	1	2	3	4	5	6	7	8
G score	2.4	2.6	3.2	3.7	4.2	4.7	5.4	6.1

The famous author Oliver Goldsmith was sometimes called Doctor Goldsmith, for he had studied medicine.

One day a poor woman asked Doctor Goldsmith to go to see her husband who was sick. Goldsmith did so. He found that the man was not only sick but very poor. There was no food in the house.

"Call at my room this evening," said Goldsmith to the woman. "I will give you some medicine for your husband."

In the evening the woman called. Goldsmith gave her a little paper box that was very heavy. When the woman opened it by her husband's side, what do you think she found? It was full of pieces of money and on the top were directions, "To be taken as often as needed." Goldsmith had given them all the money he had.

33

1. **Goldsmith had studied** Ⓐ art Ⓑ law Ⓒ music Ⓓ medicine
2. **The box was** Ⓐ light Ⓑ heavy Ⓒ flat Ⓓ deep
3. **Goldsmith told the woman to call at his** Ⓐ house Ⓑ room Ⓒ hotel Ⓓ restaurant
4. **The box was full of** Ⓐ paper Ⓑ medicine Ⓒ money Ⓓ candy
5. **The husband of the woman was** Ⓐ strong Ⓑ sick Ⓒ healthy Ⓓ tall
6. **The woman called in the** Ⓐ morning Ⓑ afternoon Ⓒ night Ⓓ evening
7. **The box was made of** Ⓐ cloth Ⓑ paper Ⓒ muslin Ⓓ satin
8. **Goldsmith was very** Ⓐ pretty Ⓑ old Ⓒ young Ⓓ kind

No. right	1	2	3	4	5	6	7	8
G score	2.3	2.5	3.0	3.5	4.0	4.6	5.4	6.1

34 Would you like to learn how to make a kite? A diamond-shaped kite is very easy to make. You must have two pieces of very light wood about as thick as a lead pencil. One piece should be thirty inches long, the other thirty-six. With your penknife make notches on both ends of both sticks. Now place the two sticks in the form of a cross and tie them together with a strong string. Join the four ends of the cross with a long string, using the notches to keep it from slipping. The frame is ready.

1. **The number of pieces of wood needed is** Ⓐ one   Ⓑ two   Ⓒ three   Ⓓ four
2. **The notches in the sticks should be** Ⓐ at one end   Ⓑ on both ends   Ⓒ in the middle   Ⓓ near the middle
3. **The lengths of the sticks should be** Ⓐ 5 inches and 6 inches   Ⓑ 10 inches and 12 inches   Ⓒ 20 inches and 24 inches   Ⓓ 30 inches and 36 inches
4. **The notches are to** Ⓐ hold the string   Ⓑ hold the paper   Ⓒ look pretty   Ⓓ hold the tail
5. **The thickness of the sticks should be about the same as a** Ⓐ needle   Ⓑ pole   Ⓒ pencil   Ⓓ pin
6. **The string should be** Ⓐ thick   Ⓑ diamond-shaped   Ⓒ 30 inches long   Ⓓ strong
7. **The sticks should be** Ⓐ tied together   Ⓑ nailed together   Ⓒ pasted together   Ⓓ sewed together
8. **Choose the best title:** Ⓐ Flying Is Fun   Ⓑ Making a Kite   Ⓒ Going Kiting   Ⓓ Tying Wood

When you have finished making the frame of the kite, get a piece of strong tissue paper. Cut it the shape of a diamond, just half an inch larger than the frame. Turn the four edges of the paper over the string and paste them. Now the main part of the kite is ready. Next make a tail. Get a piece of cord about thirty inches long. Cut some paper into small pieces, each about two inches long and one inch wide. Tie these pieces of paper onto the cord about three inches apart. This is the tail of the kite. Tie it to one of the longer tips of the diamond-shaped kite. The last thing to do is to attach the end of a ball of twine at the point where the sticks are tied together. Your kite is now ready to fly in the air.

1. **The length of the pieces of paper for the tail should be** Ⓐ 1 inch Ⓑ 2 inches Ⓒ 6 inches Ⓓ 12 inches
2. **The size of the paper to cover the frame should be** Ⓐ the same as the frame Ⓑ a little smaller than the frame Ⓒ a little larger than the frame Ⓓ much larger than the frame
3. **The length of the tail is about** Ⓐ 2 inches Ⓑ 3 inches Ⓒ 30 inches Ⓓ 36 inches
4. **Fasten the tail to** Ⓐ one of the longer tips Ⓑ one of the shorter tips Ⓒ the middle of the kite Ⓓ the side of the kite
5. **The end of a ball of twine is fastened** Ⓐ to one side Ⓑ to both sides Ⓒ to the tip Ⓓ where the sticks cross
6. **The kind of paper to use is** Ⓐ writing paper Ⓑ tissue paper Ⓒ stiff paper Ⓓ wrapping paper
7. **The paper should be fastened to the frame by** Ⓐ sewing Ⓑ nailing Ⓒ pasting Ⓓ tying
8. **The paper should be cut** Ⓐ heart-shaped Ⓑ diamond-shaped Ⓒ square Ⓓ as a circle

No. right	1	2	3	4	5	6	7	8
G score	3.8	4.3	4.7	5.3	5.8	6.3	7.0	7.5

36

Can you make a pair of scales? When I was younger, I liked to play store. One day I made some scales to weigh my groceries. I took two small round tin dishes. I made four holes around the edge of each dish. Through these holes I put strings. Then I hung a dish on each end of a short stick. I pushed a longer stick partly into the ground, balanced the shorter stick on the top of the longer one, and there was my pair of scales ready to use. I put a stone in one round tin dish and some nuts in the other. When the two tin dishes came to rest at a level, I knew that the nuts in one dish weighed the same as the stone in the other dish.

1. **When I was younger, I played**   Ⓐ horse   Ⓑ store
   Ⓒ marbles   Ⓓ games
2. **I made some scales to weigh**   Ⓐ candy   Ⓑ flour
   Ⓒ groceries   Ⓓ stones
3. **The dishes I used were**   Ⓐ china   Ⓑ round   Ⓒ square
   Ⓓ high
4. **In one dish I put some**   Ⓐ nuts   Ⓑ candies   Ⓒ sand
   Ⓓ buttons
5. **I hung the dishes on a**   Ⓐ hook   Ⓑ stick   Ⓒ tree   Ⓓ fence
6. **The strings were tied to the**   Ⓐ nuts   Ⓑ stones   Ⓒ long
   stick   Ⓓ dishes
7. **How many holes did I make in each dish?**   Ⓐ one   Ⓑ two
   Ⓒ three   Ⓓ four
8. **I wanted the scales to**   Ⓐ sing   Ⓑ balance   Ⓒ tip   Ⓓ hang
   up

No. right	1	2	3	4	5	6	7	8
G score	2.5	2.8	3.3	3.7	4.3	4.8	5.5	6.1

When I was younger, I found an opossum in the woods. I placed it in a cage and fed it for several weeks. How surprised I was one morning to see six little bare tails hanging down from the mother's pouch! Her baby opossums were inside her pouch, but all their tails were hanging outside.

One morning the baby opossums were crawling around the cage. When they saw me coming, they fled to their mother. She opened her pouch, and when they climbed inside she closed it. But their little tails could still be seen.

Later they learned not to be afraid of me. I learned that they did not like to live in my cage, so I let them go. Since opossums like night better than day, I opened the cage door just before dark. When the mother found that she was free to go, she lifted her long bare tail and stretched it along her back. Then the baby opossums climbed up on her back and wrapped their tails around her tail. They were riding like this when they all disappeared into the woods.

37

1. **This is a story chiefly about**   Ⓐ rabbits   Ⓑ opossums   Ⓒ bears   Ⓓ dogs
2. **Which time of day do opossums like best?**   Ⓐ morning   Ⓑ noon   Ⓒ afternoon   Ⓓ night
3. **How many baby opossums did this person find?**   Ⓐ two   Ⓑ four   Ⓒ six   Ⓓ eight
4. **How long was it before this person found the baby opossums? Several**   Ⓐ hours   Ⓑ days   Ⓒ weeks   Ⓓ months
5. **When the baby opossums saw this person, they were**   Ⓐ frightened   Ⓑ happy   Ⓒ curious   Ⓓ indifferent
6. **At what time of day did this person open the door of the cage?**   Ⓐ early morning   Ⓑ noon   Ⓒ near dark   Ⓓ night
7. **When the opossums left the cage, where did the mother carry her babies?**   Ⓐ in her pouch   Ⓑ on her back   Ⓒ around her neck   Ⓓ between her feet
8. **Where did the opossums go? To the**   Ⓐ bushes   Ⓑ woods   Ⓒ treetops   Ⓓ shed

No. right	1	2	3	4	5	6	7	8
G score	2.4	2.6	3.2	3.7	4.2	4.7	5.5	6.1

38

Many people enjoy making their own bread. They feel it is fresher and better for you. One interesting way to make bread is on top of the stove instead of the usual oven baking method. This way is easy because the dough doesn't need a lot of kneading. Once the molasses, flour, yeast, water, oil, and salt are mixed together, the dough is shaped into a ball. Then it is covered and put in a warm place to rise. The dough should double in size and then be punched down and allowed to rise two more times.

After it has risen the third time, the dough is placed in a heavy iron pot that has been coated with oil and sesame seeds. The pot is covered and placed over a low heat for about one hour, or until the dough bounces back when it's pushed in. The bread turns out round because the pot is round.

The best time to eat homemade bread is when it's freshly baked and still hot. With butter melted on the slices, the whole loaf disappears rapidly.

1. **According to the selection, many people make their own bread because** Ⓐ it's easier than buying it   Ⓑ it costs less   Ⓒ it's good exercise   Ⓓ it's fresher and more nutritious
2. **The usual way to bake bread is** Ⓐ in an oven   Ⓑ on top of the stove   Ⓒ in a microwave oven   Ⓓ in a fireplace
3. **The loaf disappears because** Ⓐ it is round   Ⓑ it is made with butter   Ⓒ it is delicious   Ⓓ it is covered with sesame seeds
4. **In order to rise, bread dough should be** Ⓐ covered and put in a cool place   Ⓑ uncovered and put in a cool place   Ⓒ covered and put in a warm place   Ⓓ uncovered and put in a warm place
5. **This particular kind of bread should be allowed to rise** Ⓐ 4 times   Ⓑ 1 time   Ⓒ 3 times   Ⓓ 2 times
6. **Two of the ingredients called for in making this bread are** Ⓐ pepper and salt   Ⓑ flour and yeast   Ⓒ baking soda and yeast   Ⓓ flour and sugar
7. **This bread should cook for about** Ⓐ 1 hour   Ⓑ 4 hours   Ⓒ 6 hours   Ⓓ ½ hour
8. **You know the bread is done when** Ⓐ it turns brown   Ⓑ the seeds fall off   Ⓒ the dough bounces back when it's pushed in   Ⓓ it is very hot

No. right	1	2	3	4	5	6	7	8
G score	3.4	3.7	4.0	4.4	4.7	5.2	5.6	6.1

A man had several sons who were always fighting with each other. Try as he might, he could not get them to live together in peace. He decided to show them how foolish they were. He told them to bring him a bundle of sticks. He tied the sticks together. He told each son to break the bundle across his knee. They all tried and they all failed. Then the father undid the bundle. He handed them the sticks one by one. The boys broke the sticks easily.

"You see, my boys," said the father, "when you are together, you are strong. You are more than a match for your enemies. If you quarrel and separate, you are weak and can be broken."

1. **The sons were always**   Ⓐ quarreling   Ⓑ peaceful   Ⓒ strong   Ⓓ together
2. **The father wanted to**   Ⓐ put the boys across his knee   Ⓑ teach his sons a lesson   Ⓒ fail the boys   Ⓓ separate the boys
3. **Why did the father ask for sticks?**   Ⓐ to beat the boys   Ⓑ to fight   Ⓒ to break them   Ⓓ to prove something to his sons
4. **What did the father first do with the sticks?**   Ⓐ he tied a bunch together   Ⓑ he made matches   Ⓒ he broke them across his knee   Ⓓ he tried his might
5. **When the boys tried to break the bundle, they**   Ⓐ could not do it   Ⓑ had no difficulty   Ⓒ untied them   Ⓓ used them against their enemies
6. **It was possible to break the sticks**   Ⓐ separately   Ⓑ all together in a bundle   Ⓒ in a week   Ⓓ by fighting
7. **The boys would be strong when they**   Ⓐ grew up   Ⓑ quarreled   Ⓒ separated   Ⓓ were together
8. **The father taught his sons**   Ⓐ that in union there is strength   Ⓑ to break wood   Ⓒ to use matches   Ⓓ to be enemies

No. right	1	2	3	4	5	6	7	8
G score	2.8	3.3	3.7	4.0	4.5	5.0	5.6	6.1

40

Mary once lived in a lighthouse three miles from shore. The lighthouse was built on rocks in the harbor. Mary's father kept the light burning every night so that ships would not go on the rocks and be wrecked. It was lonely out there in winter, but lots of people visited in summer. Mary liked to watch the birds fly past the lighthouse. Sometimes in the night they would fly toward the light and be killed when they struck the glass around the light. This made Mary feel sad. Now modern radio signals guide ships. Nobody lives in the lighthouse any more.

1. **The lighthouse was built**   Ⓐ on rocks   Ⓑ on the shore   Ⓒ on sand   Ⓓ in the river
2. **Mary's father kept the light burning**   Ⓐ on dark nights   Ⓑ all the time   Ⓒ every night   Ⓓ all day
3. **There is no more need for the lighthouse because**   Ⓐ there is no more danger   Ⓑ there are no more ships   Ⓒ ships now use radio signals   Ⓓ the rocks were removed
4. **The light was there to guide**   Ⓐ the rocks   Ⓑ the birds   Ⓒ Mary   Ⓓ ships
5. **In winter it was**   Ⓐ slippery   Ⓑ lonely   Ⓒ stormy   Ⓓ jolly
6. **The birds were sometimes killed by**   Ⓐ hitting against the glass   Ⓑ being burned   Ⓒ being starved   Ⓓ being shot
7. **This story makes us think that Mary was**   Ⓐ pretty   Ⓑ tall   Ⓒ merry   Ⓓ kind hearted
8. **This story shows that**   Ⓐ lighthouses have not changed   Ⓑ Mary still lives in a lighthouse   Ⓒ times have changed   Ⓓ more ships are now wrecked

No. right	1	2	3	4	5	6	7	8
G score	2.1	2.4	2.8	3.4	4.0	4.6	5.4	6.2

When we gather leaves and flowers we often want to keep them for a long time. A good way to do this is to press them. A flower press can be made out of two boards, newspapers, and a flat, heavy stone. Put a board on the bottom. On this lay several newspapers cut the same size. On top of these put the leaf or flower that you are going to press. Next, lay more newspapers on the leaf or flower. Then put the other board on top of these newspapers. Use the stone for a weight to hold the press down very firmly. Leave the leaf or flower in this press for about a week.

1. **A good way to keep leaves and flowers for a long time is to** Ⓐ put them in water Ⓑ press them Ⓒ dry them Ⓓ put them in sand
2. **How many boards do we need?** Ⓐ one Ⓑ two Ⓒ three Ⓓ six
3. **On top of the bottom board put** Ⓐ a cloth Ⓑ a leaf Ⓒ a flower Ⓓ newspapers
4. **The leaf or flower should be between** Ⓐ cloth Ⓑ cardboard Ⓒ glass Ⓓ newspapers
5. **Use the stone** Ⓐ to make the press higher Ⓑ to put under the press Ⓒ for a weight Ⓓ for a cover
6. **The leaf or flower should stay in the press about** Ⓐ an hour Ⓑ a day Ⓒ three days Ⓓ a week
7. **What sequence is given?** Ⓐ board, newspapers, flower, newspapers, board Ⓑ flowers, newspapers, flower press, stone Ⓒ flower, board, papers, stone Ⓓ board, newspapers, flower, newspapers, board, stone
8. **This story tells you** Ⓐ how to make a printing press Ⓑ uses for newspaper Ⓒ how to press leaves and flowers Ⓓ about keeping flowers fresh

No. right	1	2	3	4	5	6	7	8
G score	2.4	2.6	3.2	3.7	4.2	4.8	5.5	6.2

42

A favorite Jewish holiday is Passover. The whole family gathers for a big dinner. The father tells the story of Moses, who led the people of Israel out of Egypt.

One part of the celebration is especially fun for children. It is a game, and can be played two ways. It uses the *afikomen*, which is a piece of *matzoh*. *Matzoh* is bread which is flat and hard, because it has not risen.

In some homes, the children hide the *afikomen*. Their father has to find it. In other homes, the father hides it. When the child finds it, or the father doesn't, the *afikomen* is ransomed. The child asks for a gift. When the child and father agree on a gift, the child gives back the *afikomen* which is divided and shared. Everyone ends the meal by eating a piece.

1. A favorite Jewish holiday is   Ⓐ Mardi Gras   Ⓑ Passover   Ⓒ Columbus Day   Ⓓ Memorial Day
2. *Matzoh* is bread which is   Ⓐ flat and hard   Ⓑ brown and heavy   Ⓒ white and flabby   Ⓓ crusty
3. The *afikomen* is   Ⓐ a gift   Ⓑ a story   Ⓒ a holiday   Ⓓ a piece of *matzoh*
4. Before giving back the *afikomen*, the child asks for a   Ⓐ second *afikomen*   Ⓑ story   Ⓒ gift   Ⓓ piece to eat
5. Who tells the story of Moses?   Ⓐ the mother   Ⓑ the daughter   Ⓒ the father   Ⓓ the son
6. What happens first to the *afikomen*?   Ⓐ it is eaten   Ⓑ it is hidden   Ⓒ it is found   Ⓓ it is divided and shared
7. What happens last to the *afikomen*?   Ⓐ it is eaten   Ⓑ it is hidden   Ⓒ it is found   Ⓓ it is divided and shared
8. The story is about   Ⓐ baking bread   Ⓑ getting a gift   Ⓒ Israel and Egypt   Ⓓ a holiday game

No. right	1	2	3	4	5	6	7	8
G score	2.6	3.0	3.5	3.9	4.5	5.1	5.7	6.3

Great kick, Lakeview High! Now Smithtown's hitting long balls down the middle. But Jim's shot is blocked by Ann from Lakeview. Let's watch Randy. He's good as he takes a free kick for Lakeview. The ball's going down the line, and with a terrific shot from Eva, it's way past the post.

What's the new rage in Lakeview? It's soccer.

Teams are springing up all over America. People in other countries have loved soccer for years. In Europe, it is the favorite sport.

Last year, Randy's team was invited to Germany to play. The American students could not speak German, and the German students could not speak English, but they enjoyed playing against each other. It was also a chance to meet the people in many small towns in Germany and to promote friendship between the two countries.

---

1. **The rage in Lakeview is** Ⓐ baseball Ⓑ soccer
   Ⓒ lacrosse Ⓓ football
2. **Lakeview was playing** Ⓐ Ridgeway Ⓑ Riverside
   Ⓒ Smithtown Ⓓ Coaltown
3. **Jim was playing for** Ⓐ Smithtown Ⓑ Lakeview
   Ⓒ Germany Ⓓ Europe
4. **Randy's team was invited to** Ⓐ England Ⓑ France
   Ⓒ Italy Ⓓ Germany
5. **Who took the free kick for Lakeview?** Ⓐ Jim Ⓑ Ann
   Ⓒ Randy Ⓓ Eva
6. **Who took the last shot before the ball went past the post?**
   Ⓐ Ann Ⓑ Eva Ⓒ Randy Ⓓ Jim
7. **In Germany, the Americans could not** Ⓐ play soccer
   Ⓑ promote friendship Ⓒ visit small towns Ⓓ speak German
8. **This selection is mainly about** Ⓐ a sport Ⓑ a town in
   Germany Ⓒ a boy named Randy Ⓓ a town called Smithtown

No. right	1	2	3	4	5	6	7	8
G score	3.3	3.6	3.9	4.3	4.7	5.3	5.7	6.2

44

Outside, rain poured over the camp. Inside, Bunk Three was on an imaginary trip. Slides on a screen showed them pictures of a huge cave and they pretended they were really in it. Terry, the counselor, spoke.

"You're inside the Carlsbad Caverns. It's cool and damp in here. While some passages are narrow, some chambers are huge. You can hear your voice echo in one. Stay on the trail.

"All around you are limestone rock formations. You can see many that hang like delicate icicles. These are really very hard. And keep this in mind. None of this is made by people. Nature made this, over thousands and millions of years."

---

1. The children saw   Ⓐ movies   Ⓑ slides   Ⓒ a TV show
   Ⓓ a play

2. The weather was   Ⓐ sunny   Ⓑ windy   Ⓒ cloudy   Ⓓ rainy

3. "Imaginary" means   Ⓐ make-believe   Ⓑ real   Ⓒ funny
   Ⓓ long

4. The hanging formations were made of   Ⓐ rain   Ⓑ ice
   Ⓒ rock   Ⓓ slides

5. The caverns were made by   Ⓐ Bunk Three   Ⓑ people
   Ⓒ nature   Ⓓ Terry

6. Some passages are   Ⓐ wide   Ⓑ narrow   Ⓒ huge   Ⓓ hard

7. The name of the counselor was   Ⓐ Terry   Ⓑ Carlsbad
   Ⓒ Nature   Ⓓ Caverns

8. What is this selection about?   Ⓐ icicles   Ⓑ echoes   Ⓒ rain
   Ⓓ caverns

No. right	1	2	3	4	5	6	7	8
G score	2.4	2.7	3.3	3.7	4.3	5.0	5.7	6.4

The children watched the slide show in silence. Two large chambers in the Carlsbad Caverns reminded them of palace rooms. One resembled a forest. A large rock was named "Baby Elephant." In one chamber, some tiny rocks looked like grapes on a vine. Names had been made up for the chambers. This was called the "Grape Arbor." There were no real grapes or leaves. Everything was made of limestone.

Then there was a slide of the lunchroom, with modern tables and benches made of wood. Now the children had a joke on their counselor, Terry. "Sure, Terry," they laughed. "Nature also made this over thousands and millions of years."

1. **Some tiny rocks looked like** Ⓒ palaces Ⓓ forests Ⓔ elephants Ⓕ grapes
2. **The children were** Ⓒ silent Ⓓ noisy Ⓔ singing Ⓕ bored
3. **Which was not made of rock?** Ⓒ the grapes Ⓓ the leaves Ⓔ the tables and benches Ⓕ the baby elephant
4. **At the end, the children thought they were** Ⓒ sad Ⓓ funny Ⓔ stupid Ⓕ wet
5. **The "Baby Elephant" was** Ⓒ a large rock formation Ⓓ a real elephant Ⓔ a wooden elephant Ⓕ a toy elephant
6. **The last slide was of the** Ⓒ Grape Arbor Ⓓ Baby Elephant Ⓔ lunchroom Ⓕ camp
7. **Two chambers reminded them of** Ⓒ lunchrooms Ⓓ palace rooms Ⓔ elephants Ⓕ Terry
8. **Who was teased at the end?** Ⓒ a child Ⓓ the viewers Ⓔ an elephant Ⓕ the counselor

No. right	1	2	3	4	5	6	7	8
G score	2.5	2.9	3.5	3.8	4.4	5.0	5.6	6.3

46

Have you ever heard the phrase, "Don't rest on your laurels?"

In the days of Julius Caesar when the Roman Empire was great, there was a very special award. It was a crown made of laurel leaves. This crown had a name in Latin, the *corona civica*.

It was awarded for very brave deeds. Every soldier dreamed of winning one. You could win one if you saved the life of a fellow soldier in battle. The person who wore the crown of leaves was highly respected.

The phrase meant, "You have already won the award, but don't stop now. Go on to greater deeds."

1. **The *corona civica* was a** Ⓐ crown Ⓑ soldier Ⓒ brave deed Ⓓ great empire
2. **The crown was made of** Ⓐ silver Ⓑ gold Ⓒ bone Ⓓ leaves
3. **The phrase at the beginning meant** Ⓐ stop your work now Ⓑ go on to greater deeds Ⓒ you are a king Ⓓ don't rake the leaves
4. **The crown was awarded for** Ⓐ learning in school Ⓑ good behavior Ⓒ brave deeds Ⓓ winning a race
5. **What language gives us the words *corona civica*?** Ⓐ French Ⓑ Latin Ⓒ English Ⓓ Romanian
6. **The Roman Empire in the days of Julius Caesar was** Ⓐ a small town Ⓑ an American state Ⓒ a poor village Ⓓ a great power
7. **What kind of leaves were used for the crown?** Ⓐ maple Ⓑ oak Ⓒ laurel Ⓓ elm
8. **A person who wore the crown was** Ⓐ highly respected Ⓑ cowardly Ⓒ rich Ⓓ not liked

No. right	1	2	3	4	5	6	7	8
G score	2.5	2.8	3.4	3.8	4.4	5.1	5.7	6.4

One summer afternoon Lee and I took a walk along the edge of the cliffs. Below we saw some white spots on the ledges just above the waves. We climbed down and found to our surprise that the white spots were young sea gulls. The ledges were covered with them. They were not really white, but soft gray with brown speckles. The young gulls were not at all afraid. After running a few steps, they would stop and look at us. Some of them even let us pick them up.

Suddenly we heard the quick beat of angry wings. It was the parent birds returning. They were not as friendly as their babies and circled and darted about us. As fast as we could, we climbed back up the cliffs until the little gulls were once again white specks among the dark rocks.

47

1. **The ledges were covered with** Ⓐ eggs   Ⓑ young gulls Ⓒ shells   Ⓓ moss
2. **The parent birds returned** Ⓐ to eat their dinner   Ⓑ to walk on the rocks   Ⓒ to protect their babies   Ⓓ to roost for the night
3. **Lee and I went for a walk in the** Ⓐ morning   Ⓑ evening Ⓒ forenoon   Ⓓ afternoon
4. **The young gulls were not** Ⓐ friendly   Ⓑ afraid   Ⓒ tame Ⓓ hungry
5. **At a distance the little gulls looked like** Ⓐ baby birds   Ⓑ tiny eggs   Ⓒ white specks   Ⓓ dark rocks
6. **The parent birds** Ⓐ lighted on the rocks   Ⓑ circled and darted   Ⓒ fed their young   Ⓓ swam in water
7. **We went away** Ⓐ slowly   Ⓑ down the cliff   Ⓒ in our boat Ⓓ as fast as we could
8. **Choose the best title:** Ⓐ Summer   Ⓑ A Walk   Ⓒ A Sea Gull Nursery   Ⓓ The Cliffs

No. right	1	2	3	4	5	6	7	8
G score	2.4	2.7	3.3	3.8	4.4	5.1	5.8	6.7

48

The mole has a very strange way of digging his tunnels. He has a long, pointed nose which extends far beyond his mouth. It is very hard and he uses it to bore into the earth. He uses his short, wide forefeet like shovels to push the earth back. He works very fast and is one of the best diggers in the animal world.

In cold or dry weather he tunnels deep underground. There is a reason for this. It is then that the worms and grubs, which are his food, go deep into the earth and he follows. In warm weather you can see the earth rise in a little ridge as he makes his tunnel near the surface.

1. **The mole works** Ⓐ slowly   Ⓑ quickly   Ⓒ carelessly   Ⓓ lazily
2. **The end of his nose is**   Ⓐ soft   Ⓑ wet   Ⓒ hard   Ⓓ dry
3. **His forefeet are**   Ⓐ small and pointed   Ⓑ long and narrow   Ⓒ bare and white   Ⓓ short and wide
4. **He uses his nose to**   Ⓐ smell his enemies   Ⓑ find his way   Ⓒ bore into the ground   Ⓓ fight
5. **He pushes back the earth with his**   Ⓐ back legs   Ⓑ tail   Ⓒ nose   Ⓓ forefeet
6. **The mole is called a**   Ⓐ climber   Ⓑ digger   Ⓒ jumper   Ⓓ swimmer
7. **He digs deeper into the ground in**   Ⓐ cold weather   Ⓑ warm weather   Ⓒ wet weather   Ⓓ any weather
8. **His food is mostly**   Ⓐ flies   Ⓑ roots   Ⓒ grains and seeds   Ⓓ worms and grubs

No. right	1	2	3	4	5	6	7	8
G score	2.3	2.6	3.2	3.7	4.3	5.0	5.8	6.6

Mr. Walker rocked on his porch. This was his vacation, and his whole family was at their beach house.

A little boy came by. Scooter, who was only five, lived next door. He liked to visit Joanie and Beth, who were eight and nine. "Hi, Mr. Walker!" he said. "I brought some cookies for Joanie and Beth!"

The next day Scooter came again. This time he brought some peaches. The third day he brought sandwiches. The fourth day he brought leftover meat.

Then on the fifth day, Scooter came with cold spaghetti for Joanie and Beth.

"I saved this from my lunch," he said. "Is it enough? I hope you won't be hungry."

"We're not hungry," the girls said. "Why are you worried?"

"Because you don't have any food!" Scooter said.

"Why do you think that?" Beth asked.

"My father goes to work every day," Scooter said, "He says that if he stays home, we won't have any food in the house. But your father stays home. So you and Joanie must be starving."

Everyone laughed. Then Mr. Walker explained about vacations.

49

1. **Mr. Walker's family was at** Ⓐ their beach house Ⓑ Scooter's house Ⓒ a forest cabin Ⓓ a hotel

2. **Who was the youngest?** Ⓐ Joanie Ⓑ Beth Ⓒ Scooter Ⓓ Mr. Walker

3. **Who went to work every day?** Ⓐ Mr. Walker Ⓑ Scooter's father Ⓒ Scooter Ⓓ Joanie and Beth

4. **On the fifth day, Scooter brought** Ⓐ peaches Ⓑ cold spaghetti Ⓒ cookies Ⓓ sandwiches

5. **Scooter thought that** Ⓐ Joanie went to work Ⓑ Mr. Walker went to work Ⓒ his father was hungry Ⓓ Joanie and Beth had no food in the house

6. **Scooter was** Ⓐ a boy who was hungry Ⓑ a boy who was eight years old Ⓒ a boy who was unfriendly Ⓓ a boy who cared

7. **On the first day, Scooter brought** Ⓐ peaches Ⓑ cold spaghetti Ⓒ cookies Ⓓ sandwiches

8. **Scooter lived** Ⓐ next door to the Walkers Ⓑ down the hill Ⓒ in a city Ⓓ above the Walkers

No. right	1	2	3	4	5	6	7	8
G score	3.0	3.5	3.8	4.4	5.0	5.6	6.2	7.0

50

Have you ever thought how necessary trees are to us? Trees give us fruit and nuts to eat, wood to use for fuel, and timber for buildings and furniture. From them we also get cork, turpentine, rubber, and maple sugar. Much of our paper is made from wood. The shade of the trees keeps the sun from drying the ground. The tree roots laced together hold the soil so that rainstorms cannot wash it away. Tree roots also hold the water in the ground and protect places where springs and brooks begin. If a hillside or other piece of land is stripped of trees, the nearby springs and brooks often dry up entirely. That is why the nation has employed thousands of people to plant or protect millions of trees.

1. **Some of the foods that we get from trees are** Ⓐ fruits and vegetables Ⓑ nuts and rubber Ⓒ fruits and nuts Ⓓ fruits and timber
2. **Timber is used for** Ⓐ maple sugar Ⓑ rubber Ⓒ turpentine Ⓓ buildings and furniture
3. **We get turpentine from** Ⓐ plants Ⓑ mines Ⓒ trees Ⓓ animals
4. **The roots of trees keep the soil** Ⓐ broken apart Ⓑ dry Ⓒ together Ⓓ warm
5. **On a treeless hillside the soil is very likely to be** Ⓐ very fertile Ⓑ very wet Ⓒ washed away Ⓓ very sandy
6. **The shade keeps the ground from** Ⓐ drying out Ⓑ washing away Ⓒ getting too wet Ⓓ getting too sandy
7. **The story shows us** Ⓐ how to care for trees Ⓑ why trees are valuable Ⓒ how to plant trees Ⓓ why we should plant fruit trees
8. **Choose the best title:** Ⓐ The Importance of Trees Ⓑ Soil and Water Ⓒ Timber Ⓓ Planters of Trees

No. right	1	2	3	4	5	6	7	8
G score	2.7	3.2	3.6	4.1	4.6	5.2	5.8	6.5

Real chewing gum is made from the sap of the sapodilla tree. The sapodilla grows in the tropics of South America. This sap is called chicle. When chewing gum is made, flavorings are added to the chicle as it is melted. Then the gum is rolled through a sheeting machine. Then the sheets are chopped up into sticks of gum. Scientists believe cave men used to chew gum. Their gum was just the sticky resin from spruce trees. American Indians used to chew this resin too. They introduced it to the pioneers. Then the early settlers started chewing refined paraffin. People found out about chicle through Mexico. In 1869, William and Semple patented chicle gum. Today, the U.S. is still the largest producer of chewing gum, but gum is also made in many other countries.

1. **The sap from the sapodilla tree is called**   Ⓐ resin   Ⓑ raisin   Ⓒ chiclets   Ⓓ chicle
2. **Real chewing gum is made from**   Ⓐ sapodilla leaves   Ⓑ paraffin   Ⓒ chicle   Ⓓ resin
3. **What is added to chicle?**   Ⓐ chewing gum   Ⓑ sticky resin   Ⓒ flavorings   Ⓓ sap
4. **After the gum is rolled flat, it is**   Ⓐ eaten   Ⓑ melted   Ⓒ cut into sticks   Ⓓ flavored
5. **Sapodilla trees grow in**   Ⓐ the U.S.   Ⓑ India   Ⓒ South America   Ⓓ all parts of the world
6. **Early settlers chewed**   Ⓐ chicle   Ⓑ spruce tree resin   Ⓒ paraffin   Ⓓ sapodilla
7. **Chicle gum was patented in**   Ⓐ 1869 by William Semple   Ⓑ 1869 by William and Semple   Ⓒ 1896 by Wm. Semple   Ⓓ 1896 by William & Semple
8. **Who introduced gum to the pioneers?**   Ⓐ cave men   Ⓑ scientists   Ⓒ William and Semple   Ⓓ Indians

No. right	1	2	3	4	5	6	7	8
G score	3.4	3.7	4.2	4.6	5.1	5.6	6.2	6.8

52

In Europe, a royal wedding takes place. Now we can watch it "live"—as it happens—on television in America. People in Europe can watch our "live" shows also. This was not possible before the 1960s.

Special satellites make it possible. A famous early one is called *Telstar*. A giant rocket launches the satellite. It goes into orbit around the earth. The earth is turning also. The satellite follows the rotation of the earth. In this way, it stays over the same place.

Let's say the show is coming from England to America. In England, a station beams a signal to the satellite. The satellite picks up the signal and makes it stronger. Then it sends the signal down to a station in America. We see a clear picture on our television screens.

These satellites are called *communications satellites*. They are used not only for television, but for telephone calls, radio, and other kinds of messages.

1. **People in Europe could not watch American shows "live" before**
   Ⓐ the 1920s   Ⓑ the 1940s   Ⓒ the 1960s   Ⓓ the 1980s
2. **We watch a "live" show**   Ⓐ as it happens   Ⓑ before it happens   Ⓒ the day after it happens   Ⓓ a week after it happens
3. **An early communications satellite is**   Ⓐ the moon   Ⓑ Venus   Ⓒ Mars   Ⓓ Telstar
4. **A giant rocket launches**   Ⓐ the television   Ⓑ the satellite   Ⓒ the signal   Ⓓ the station
5. **The satellite goes into orbit**   Ⓐ around the sun   Ⓑ around the moon   Ⓒ around the earth   Ⓓ around Venus
6. **On earth, a station beams a signal**   Ⓐ to another station   Ⓑ to a television screen   Ⓒ to a giant rocket   Ⓓ to the special satellite
7. **The satellite sends the signal**   Ⓐ down to another station   Ⓑ back to the first station   Ⓒ to the moon   Ⓓ to another planet
8. **The satellite can stay over the same place on earth because**   Ⓐ the satellite and the earth aren't moving   Ⓑ both are moving in the same direction   Ⓒ the satellite alone stays still   Ⓓ the earth alone stays still

No. right	1	2	3	4	5	6	7	8
G score	2.7	3.3	3.7	4.1	4.6	5.3	5.8	6.5

Can you take good photos? Is this your first camera? Why not learn from my mistakes? Look over my photos.

1. See these little ants? One is Aunt Sue. One is Aunt Jane. Here are Uncle Tom and my three cousins. I stood too far away.
2. Here are my friends. This time I shook the camera. That's why everyone is fuzzy. I have to guess who's who.
3. This is my sister's tee shirt. My sister was wearing it at the time. But when I looked through the view finder, I was careless. That's why it looks as if her head is chopped off. Always make sure you see people's heads when you take pictures of them.
4. Here is a picture of my finger. By accident, I rested it over the lens. With some simple cameras, it's easy to make this mistake. The view finder won't tell you.

Think ahead and enjoy your photos!

1. **The writer shows us** Ⓐ one picture Ⓑ two pictures Ⓒ three pictures Ⓓ four pictures
2. **This selection** Ⓐ gives advice Ⓑ tells a story Ⓒ teaches a recipe Ⓓ teaches us history
3. **This selection is mainly about** Ⓐ making tee shirts Ⓑ taking good photos Ⓒ friends Ⓓ cousins
4. **One picture was too fuzzy because the writer** Ⓐ stood too far away Ⓑ rested a finger over the lens Ⓒ didn't see the head Ⓓ shook the camera
5. **You will take a picture of your finger if you** Ⓐ stand too far away Ⓑ rest your finger over the lens Ⓒ shake the camera Ⓓ wear a tee shirt
6. **How did the sister look?** Ⓐ as if her head were chopped off Ⓑ fuzzy Ⓒ like an ant Ⓓ like a finger
7. **In picture #1, the relatives looked like** Ⓐ birds Ⓑ fingers Ⓒ ants Ⓓ kittens
8. **What is the view finder for?** Ⓐ looking through Ⓑ pressing Ⓒ holding Ⓓ making mistakes

No. right	1	2	3	4	5	6	7	8
G score	3.3	3.7	4.0	4.6	5.1	5.6	6.2	6.9

54

A thirsty crow found a pitcher with some water in it, but there was so little that the crow could not reach it with her beak. It seemed that she would die of thirst within sight of what could save her. At last she hit upon a clever plan. She began dropping pebbles into the pitcher. With each pebble, the water rose a little higher until it reached the brim. The knowing bird was able to quench her thirst.

1. **What did the crow need?** Ⓐ a pitcher Ⓑ a pebble Ⓒ food Ⓓ a drink
2. **What would save her?** Ⓐ the water she could see Ⓑ the sea of water Ⓒ a rose Ⓓ the brim of the pitcher
3. **Why didn't she drink the water right away?** Ⓐ it was full of pebbles Ⓑ her beak was too short Ⓒ she died of thirst Ⓓ the water was dirty
4. **Why didn't she break the pitcher?** Ⓐ she was stupid Ⓑ the water would spill Ⓒ she quenched her thirst Ⓓ it was within sight
5. **How did the crow know what to do?** Ⓐ she thought of an idea Ⓑ someone told her Ⓒ she knew all along Ⓓ she read a clever plan
6. **What happened when the crow dropped pebbles in the water?** Ⓐ she hit a plan Ⓑ the water got higher Ⓒ they broke the pitcher Ⓓ roses grew
7. **Which word does not tell about the crow?** Ⓐ thirsty Ⓑ intelligent Ⓒ resourceful Ⓓ high
8. **Choose the best title:** Ⓐ How to Hit a Plan Ⓑ Necessity Is the Mother of Invention Ⓒ Stones and Crows Ⓓ Clean Pebbles

No. right	1	2	3	4	5	6	7	8
G score	2.4	2.8	3.4	3.9	4.6	5.3	6.0	6.8

A city farmer tried to grow vegetables in soil for the first time. In his back yard he planned to grow radishes, lettuce, cabbage, and beans. He bought the seeds and planted them. Every day he went to see if they had come up. The bright sun and then the warm rain caused them to grow very quickly. The man was pleased with everything except the beans.

"I shall never try to grow beans again," he said one day to his neighbor, who was also out in his garden. "The seeds won't stay in the ground. Only this morning I had to cover them all again." What do you think the neighbor told him?

1. **The seeds were planted in** Ⓐ a flower-pot   Ⓑ the front yard
   Ⓒ the back yard   Ⓓ a window box
2. **The garden was planted with** Ⓐ vegetables   Ⓑ flowers
   Ⓒ fruit   Ⓓ berries
3. **This man needed to study** Ⓐ carpentry   Ⓑ gardening
   Ⓒ painting   Ⓓ buying and selling
4. **What the man did not know was** Ⓐ how to plant beans   Ⓑ the
   way to water his garden   Ⓒ that bean seeds are pushed above the
   ground   Ⓓ how to cover the beans
5. **The way the beans grew made the man** Ⓐ angry   Ⓑ happy
   Ⓒ contented   Ⓓ discouraged
6. **He told his troubles to his** Ⓐ son   Ⓑ wife   Ⓒ father
   Ⓓ neighbor
7. **The best thing for the neighbor to tell him was to** Ⓐ buy better
   seed   Ⓑ leave the plants alone   Ⓒ keep covering them
   Ⓓ plant the seeds deeper
8. **The sunshine and rain** Ⓐ killed the plants   Ⓑ helped the plants
   grow   Ⓒ ruined the beans   Ⓓ stayed in the ground

No. right	1	2	3	4	5	6	7	8
G score	2.2	2.5	3.2	3.8	4.7	5.7	6.8	7.8

56

Guess what I am! In springtime I come out of my warm winter home in a rotting log and dig a hole in the ground. After that, I gather pollen and make a bed of it in the hole. On this bed I lay eggs that I sit on until they hatch as larvae. After eating the pollen, the larvae spin webs around themselves and go to sleep for a few days. Then my little gray babies come out of their cocoons and crawl under my furry body for warmth and protection.

When their bodies become streaked with orange, they are ready to go to work. And how they work! From dawn to dark and even in the moonlight! They fly everywhere to gather honey, pollen, and other nest material. They have no fear, for each has a sharp stinger. By the time winter comes, all have worked themselves to death. Only the queens live on. They go to their lonely winter homes. What am I?

1. **This is a story of** Ⓐ bears Ⓑ insects Ⓒ flies Ⓓ birds
2. **Members of my family are ready to work when they are streaked with** Ⓐ blue Ⓑ red Ⓒ yellow Ⓓ orange
3. **Which members of this family live longest?** Ⓐ workers Ⓑ strongest ones Ⓒ queens Ⓓ kings
4. **After they have eaten the pollen, the larvae** Ⓐ grow wings Ⓑ spin webs around themselves Ⓒ crawl under my body Ⓓ start to build a main nest
5. **In this story, where was my winter home? In a** Ⓐ bush Ⓑ log Ⓒ house Ⓓ hole in the ground
6. **My springtime home is located in a** Ⓐ tree Ⓑ hollow log Ⓒ hole in the ground Ⓓ bird cage
7. **I lay my eggs on a bed of** Ⓐ dry leaves Ⓑ dirt Ⓒ grass Ⓓ pollen
8. **These insects are** Ⓐ very lazy Ⓑ very fearful Ⓒ hard working Ⓓ unprotected

Do you like strawberry jam on your toast? If so, you might like to make your own. It's not hard. To do this, you will need the following: 4 cups of sliced strawberries; ⅓ cup of sugar; 2 tablespoons of lemon juice; one envelope of unflavored gelatin; and ½ cup of cold water.

Start by mixing the strawberries, the sugar, and the lemon juice in a medium-sized pan. Heat this mixture gently for 5 minutes. Crush the strawberries slightly as you heat them. Then, turn up the heat and boil the mixture for 3 minutes. Stir the mixture while it boils.

Pour the water into a small bowl. Then sprinkle the gelatin over the water. Pour the water and gelatin into the strawberry mixture. Then heat and stir the new mixture until the gelatin dissolves.

Now turn off the stove and let the jam stand for 5 minutes. As it cools, remove the foam which forms on the top. Next, use a big spoon to move the jam from the pan into glass jars. Cover the jars and let them cool off. Finally, put the jars in the refrigerator. Your jam is ready for tomorrow morning.

57

---

1. **To make strawberry jam you will need** Ⓐ one cup of cold water Ⓑ four cups of sugar Ⓒ four tablespoons of lemon juice Ⓓ four cups of sliced strawberries
2. **The gelatin you use should be** Ⓐ lemon flavored Ⓑ unflavored Ⓒ sugar flavored Ⓓ strawberry flavored
3. **The first step is to** Ⓐ crush the strawberries Ⓑ heat the strawberries Ⓒ boil the strawberries Ⓓ mix the strawberries, sugar, and lemon juice
4. **You are to boil the mixture of strawberries** Ⓐ 3 minutes Ⓑ five minutes Ⓒ until the gelatin dissolves Ⓓ 8 minutes
5. **You are to add the gelatin** Ⓐ after adding the water Ⓑ together with the water Ⓒ before adding the water Ⓓ to the sugar
6. **You are to let the jam stand in order to** Ⓐ let the gelatin dissolve Ⓑ let the foam form Ⓒ keep it from exploding Ⓓ kill any germs
7. **Right after you put the jam in jars, you are supposed to** Ⓐ freeze it Ⓑ leave the jars open Ⓒ let it cool Ⓓ heat it again
8. **The jam made using this recipe** Ⓐ must be frozen Ⓑ must be used right away Ⓒ should be refrigerated Ⓓ is foamy

No. right	1	2	3	4	5	6	7	8
G score	3.9	4.3	4.7	5.1	5.6	6.0	6.5	7.0

58

Seeing eye dogs, or guide dogs, lead very interesting lives. For ten or twelve years, or even longer, they are responsible for leading a blind person. To do this job, they must be intelligent, gentle, and very well trained.

Most guide dogs are born at a kennel. Since dogs are gentler when they are raised by a family, the dogs are given to children. When the dogs are about fourteen months old, they come back to the kennel to be trained, and the children get new puppies.

The dogs train in groups of six or eight for three months. They know more at the end of that time than most dogs ever learn. But the training isn't over. Their new masters arrive and they train together for one more month. At the end of that time, they are ready for the world.

A dog loves nothing better than to be with its master, and guide dogs keep their masters company all the time.

---

1. **Another name for a seeing eye dog is** Ⓐ blind dog Ⓑ German shepherd Ⓒ guide dog Ⓓ master
2. **Seeing eye dogs must be** Ⓐ fierce Ⓑ well trained Ⓒ playful Ⓓ fast runners
3. **Dogs are gentler if they are** Ⓐ in a kennel Ⓑ twelve years old Ⓒ intelligent Ⓓ raised by a family
4. **Guide dogs train at the kennel for** Ⓐ 6 months Ⓑ 14 months Ⓒ 4 months Ⓓ 8 months
5. **When a guide dog is a year old, it** Ⓐ starts training Ⓑ has finished training Ⓒ is with a blind master Ⓓ is still with a family
6. **Seeing eye dogs train with their masters for** Ⓐ 1 month Ⓑ 1 year Ⓒ 4 months Ⓓ 14 months
7. **At first, how do the dogs train?** Ⓐ with a family Ⓑ with their masters Ⓒ in groups Ⓓ with blind people
8. **Guide dogs learn** Ⓐ more than most dogs Ⓑ how to attack Ⓒ to see in the dark Ⓓ to follow their masters

No. right	1	2	3	4	5	6	7	8
G score	3.3	3.7	4.0	4.4	4.9	5.4	5.9	6.5

Have you ever heard the song, *Casey Jones*? It's about an engineer who worked on the Illinois Central Railroad. His real name was John Luther Jones, but when he was a telegraph operator in Cayce, Kentucky, he got the nickname Casey.

Casey Jones used to boast that he could always get the train in on time. Then he got a chance to be the engineer on the Cannon Ball Express. That passenger train went from Memphis, Tennessee, to Canton, Mississippi. It was a good train, but there had been many accidents on that run because the tracks were so dangerous. When Casey picked up the train in Memphis, it was already late. He wanted to keep his promise to bring the train in on time. That promise led to disaster.

At Vaughan, Mississippi, Casey saw a freight train standing on the tracks right in front of the speeding Cannon Ball Express. It was too late to stop. He ordered the workman on the train with him to jump. He put on the brakes. On the morning of April 30, 1900, the Cannon Ball Express smashed into the freight train, killing Casey Jones. Because he had stayed at his post, all the passengers were saved.

59

---

1. **Casey Jones's real name was**   Ⓐ Vaughan Jones   Ⓑ Cayce Jones   Ⓒ John Luther Jones   Ⓓ James Earl Jones
2. **Before he was an engineer, Casey was a**   Ⓐ telephone operator   Ⓑ singer   Ⓒ telegraph operator   Ⓓ song writer
3. **Casey Jones liked his train to be**   Ⓐ punctual   Ⓑ the fastest   Ⓒ cautious   Ⓓ shiny
4. **Casey worked for**   Ⓐ Mississippi Railroad   Ⓑ Northern Central   Ⓒ Memphis Central   Ⓓ Illinois Central
5. **The Cannon Ball Express usually went from Memphis to**   Ⓐ Cayce, Kentucky   Ⓑ Central Illinois   Ⓒ Canton, Miss.   Ⓓ St. Louis, Mo.
6. **The Cannon Ball Express was a**   Ⓐ freight train   Ⓑ passenger train   Ⓒ local train   Ⓓ electric train
7. **Casey Jones died on**   Ⓐ April 30, 1800   Ⓑ May 30, 1900   Ⓒ May 30, 1800   Ⓓ April 30, 1900
8. **The passengers were saved because**   Ⓐ Casey ordered them to jump   Ⓑ Casey died   Ⓒ they got out of the way   Ⓓ Casey put on the brakes

No. right	1	2	3	4	5	6	7	8
G score	3.5	3.9	4.4	5.0	5.6	6.2	6.9	7.4

60

My grandfather says that he once met an old sailor. The man had only one eye. When grandfather met him, the sailor was dying. The sailor told him that he had sailed with the famous pirate Molly Mingo. He said that he had even helped Molly bury a large treasure. Later, a British war ship caught the pirates. All the pirates, except the one-eyed sailor, were killed in the battle. The sailor was captured and put in jail.

The old sailor told Grandfather that the treasure was buried on Platero Island. "Go to Frenchman's Bay," he said. "There you will find a square, blue rock. Walk south one hundred steps from the blue rock. Then, go east the length of a long boat. There, you will see a very old banyan tree. Climb to the top of this tree and look south. You will see a small hill. On top of this hill is a pointed rock. Behind it is another hill. In the side of the other hill is a cave. The cave is right in line with the tip of the rock. The treasure is in the cave."

I have never been to Platero Island so I don't know if this story is true. It may just be one of Grandfather's stories, but if you ever get there, you might take a look.

1. **The author's grandfather** Ⓐ sailed with Molly Mingo Ⓑ met an old sailor Ⓒ found Molly's treasure Ⓓ buried Molly's treasure
2. **The old sailor** Ⓐ had one eye Ⓑ helped catch Molly Mingo Ⓒ had one arm Ⓓ found the treasure
3. **When the pirates were caught how many were killed?** Ⓐ one Ⓑ all except one Ⓒ none Ⓓ all of them
4. **In Frenchman's Bay you will find** Ⓐ the treasure Ⓑ a pointed rock Ⓒ an old long boat Ⓓ a blue rock
5. **You are supposed to walk south one hundred steps from the** Ⓐ banyan tree Ⓑ long boat Ⓒ small hill Ⓓ blue rock
6. **You can see the pointed rock from the top of the** Ⓐ blue rock Ⓑ bay Ⓒ banyan tree Ⓓ cave
7. **The cave is** Ⓐ under the pointed rock Ⓑ in the second hill Ⓒ near the banyan tree Ⓓ north of the pointed rock
8. **According to the author** Ⓐ the story is true Ⓑ the story is not true Ⓒ the story might not be true Ⓓ he plans to look for the treasure

No. right	1	2	3	4	5	6	7	8
G score	2.7	3.4	3.9	4.6	5.3	6.1	7.0	7.7